For Better or Worse

The Legacy of William "Deadshot" Reed

For Better or Worse

The Legacy of William "Deadshot" Reed

Kathy Deinhardt Hill

Big Mallard
Books
McCall, Idaho

Published by
Big Mallard Books
14068 Pioneer Road
McCall, Idaho 83638
(208) 634-1062

Photos provided by the Reed family except where noted.

Edited by Frances Ford
Illustrations by Amber Strickler

ISBN: 0-9717256-1-6

LCCN: 2003091288

To Anne and Ruth,
who told me the stories

Table of Contents

Prologue

When William Reed rode into Idaho in the early 1900s, he carried with him a pocketful of stories, enough to mask his ruthless past and give him a fresh start. He changed his name and his occupation and settled in the rugged area around Pierce, Idaho, ninety-five miles northeast of Lewiston. But trouble, like a stalker, tracked Reed. Within three years of his arrival in Idaho, he ran afoul of the law, involved in a cattle rustling scheme that led to an ambush that killed his partner. Reed, too, was shot in the melee, his right arm shattered beyond repair.

He escaped jail time, but angered an entire community when he eloped with a fourteen-year old beauty, Bessie Warren. What followed was a forty-eight year marriage that endured itinerant wandering, more run-ins with the law, and twelve children, many of them born on the South Fork of the Salmon River at a place now known as the Reed Ranch.

His demeanor and his behavior led people to invent incredible stories about the wiry man from Texas; he did little to dissuade them. They whispered about his hidden past, and what little he revealed about himself sparked even more interest. His quick temper, supported by his handiwork with a gun, became legendary. People crossed to the other side of the street when they saw "Deadshot" heading their way, his Colt .45 riding on his hip.

To his children, he was demanding and cruel, a man to be feared rather than loved. He was also a mystery; the cryptic stories he told them, with vague references to distant people and places, left them guessing. Even his beloved Bessie, the only person who saw the good in him, the only person who could calm him, was unable to unlock William Reed's secrets.

Life with William Reed was not easy, and as soon as they could, most of his children left home to escape his threats and his control. Many were reluctant to discuss their father, preferring to forget the torment he caused, sharing only bits and pieces of their lives with this intense, unpredictable man. Bessie also refused to discuss the dark side of her husband. A 1964 manuscript about Deadshot went unpublished when Bessie objected to the work which she believed showed Reed as an "undesirable, bad man."

But the tale of Deadshot Reed needs to be told, and told as accurately as the record will allow. It relates the turbulent life of the gunslinger and his resilient wife and her efforts to raise her family despite incredible odds. It recounts both the joy and the tragedy of a family struggling to overcome not only Idaho's rugged back country in the early 1900s, but also the violent temper and roguish reputation of the family's leader. The story of Deadshot Reed is clearly a memorable and colorful part of central Idaho's history.

1

Trouble from Texas

Nothing was ordinary about William Reed. Only five feet, five inches tall, William Reed's small stature belied his mean streak and maybe even had a hand in creating it. He had ice blue eyes, cold and cruel; they won every stare down and allowed him to back down to no one. He dressed meticulously in the attire of a cowboy, complete with hat and boots, which added height to his lean, compact stature. He wore his thick, dark hair shortly cropped, and it went well with his weathered complexion. Clean shaven, except for a full mustache which extended from his top lip down the corners of his mouth, Reed exuded confidence, arrogance, superiority. Pictures of Reed reveal an intense man, staring right into the camera with an angry, impenetrable look. When he rode into Idaho in 1905, it was clear he carried a heavy chip on his shoulder, and he dared all he met to knock it off.

Little is known about Reed before he came to Idaho, and what we do know comes from Reed himself. A masterful story-teller who could enthrall both men and children, he brewed a tale of bravery and treachery, action and mystery, which his listeners absorbed in wonder. From the stories about a young boy who shot his teacher, to those of a Texas Ranger and a sharp-shooter in a wild west show, to those of a poker-playing miner in the Klondike gold rush, Reed's life prior to his arrival in Idaho is anyone's guess. If only half of the stories he told were true, William Reed was both remarkable and notorious.

Exactly when Reed was born is uncertain because he admitted to lying about his age to get into the Texas Rangers. Once he arrived in Idaho, however, Reed was consistent in claiming he was born in Texas on July 5, 1876. This date appears on his marriage license, his World War I draft record, and his death certificate.

Reed always said he was from Texas, although he never made clear exactly where in Texas he called home. Most of the time, he claimed he was from San Antonio—San *Antone,* he would say, when talking to his friends. He also told others he missed the Cherokee Strip, land of his boyhood, except that the Cherokee Strip is part of Oklahoma, not Texas. It was on the Cherokee Strip in 1893 that the great Oklahoma land rush took place, where thousands of would-be ranchers and farmers made a mad dash for free land and part of the American Dream. Reed would have been seventeen at the time, so it is possible he was involved in this land grab; however, during this time, Reed said he was performing with a wild west show.

The story commonly held as true was the one he told his wife Bessie; he was born in Graham, Young County, Texas, 300 miles north of San Antonio, 250 miles south of the Cherokee Strip. Whether or not William Reed was his true name is unknown; his family believes he chose the name after fleeing Texas. Throughout the years, variations of this name appear in Idaho records. Between 1905 and 1912 while in Pierce and northern Idaho, he went by William P. Reed, although sometimes spelling his last name R*ei*d. When he arrived on the South Fork of the Salmon River in central Idaho, he changed his name to William Lee Reed, telling his children that Lee was his mother's maiden name. He added that she was a descendant of Robert E. Lee, the great Confederate general. However on his World War I draft registration in 1918, Reed indicated his middle name was Lane. This is the only time this name appears on any public record. In subsequent legal documents, Reed used the initial L. or Lee as his middle name.

Thus, because of this probable assumed name and his propensity to stretch the truth, it is impossible to trace Reed's roots. He alleged his father, George, was killed in a fight over a horse race, leaving his mother, Maggie, to raise the family, which consisted of Reed, his two brothers, Allison and George, and his sister Anna. However, 1880 census records from Texas reveal no families anywhere in Texas with those specific family members. Reed also claimed that his uncle owned one of the largest horse ranches in Texas; another uncle, or perhaps the same one, served as the sheriff of a Texas county. Again, no public records can confirm his stories.

In Reed's later years, he often hinted he was related to the Henry Hill family of Sweet, Idaho. Henry Hill came to Idaho from Texas in the 1890s. A direct link from a Maggie Hill in Young County, Texas, can be traced to this Hill family in Sweet. On February 17, 1875, Maggie Hill married Thomas Harrington in Young County and in 1884, eight year old John J. Harrington was attending school there. Whether or not John J. Harrington grew up to become William Reed is strictly conjecture and cannot be determined.

What we do know for certain is that at a young age, Reed took an interest in guns. Perhaps this interest came from the culture in which he lived or because of his small stature and the need to defend himself. By the time he arrived in Idaho, he was more than proficient with both pistol and rifle, and he used both with lightening speed and precision.

If Reed's account of his boyhood is true, where he lived on a ranch working with cattle, where arguments were settled with fists and guns, he would have learned early that a gun was a necessity for survival. He also would have figured out that the man who was willing to use his gun and use it well would have an advantage. He was still a boy when he applied this adage.

According to the story Reed told his family, he was twelve years old when he killed his first victim, his school teacher. Reed claimed the man had it coming, and in his later years, he blamed his propensity for violence on this teacher.

The alleged shooting occurred just after lunch, in a one-room school house on the outskirts of San Antonio. As with most schools of the 1880s, boys and girls were separated during recess and lunch time. When an errant ball landed at the feet of a young, handsome Bill Reed, he decided to return it personally to the girl who threw it. He climbed the fence separating the two playgrounds and proceeded to talk to the girl. All the while, the head teacher had his watchful eye focused on Reed. When the lunch break was over, the teacher informed Reed he had broken the rules. He was told to stand firm and take his beating. The teacher struck Reed once on the forearm; Reed told him to stop, but the teacher ignored him and hit him again. When he raised the cane a third time, Reed pulled a pistol and fired one shot at the teacher, killing him.

Over the years, this story has remained relatively consistent, although acquaintances of Reed have contributed varying details, apparently added around campfires on hunting and trapping trips. Art Colson, in his work *Rewards of Rage,* claims Reed was fourteen at the time of the shooting. According to Colson, Reed had climbed the school's playground fence to share his lunch with his sister and was caught by the head teacher. When the teacher informed Reed of his impending punishment, Reed shot him before the teacher even raised his hand. Later, when Reed recalled the incident, he said he regretted his first killing, as it "changed his life forever."

Following the shooting, Reed escaped. He told his children he ran to his uncle, the sheriff of a nearby county. Colson writes that Reed sought safety with an uncle who owned a big ranch. Whatever the case, the uncle gave Reed money and instructions to get out of the country, which he did, fleeing to South America.

Reed never spoke of South America to his family. It is unclear exactly how long he stayed there, although Colson states it was six years. Reed was fluent in Spanish by the time he arrived in Idaho, an aptitude he never explained. He may have learned it living in South America, but it is also possible he learned the language while in Texas.

Based on what Reed told his family, Colson's estimate of six years in South America is out of line. If Reed stayed out of the country for six years, he would have returned to the United States in 1894, when he was around eighteen years old. However, Reed told his family that on his return to the United States, he changed his name, lied about his age, and joined the Texas Rangers, where he served for two years. Following that, he was employed by the Union Metallic Cartridge Company, touring in wild west shows, including one at the 1893 World's Fair in Chicago. This age discrepancy is unexplainable.

As a Texas Ranger, Reed fit the persona he created for himself. Bigger than life, bigger than the law itself, many of the men who rode with the Rangers became legends in their heroic pursuit of justice on the plains of Texas.

The purpose of the Rangers was to protect settlers in Texas from Comanchee Indians. Originally established in 1823 by the Mexican government and under the authority of Stephen F. Austin, over the year the Rangers would undergo many changes under the direction of Mexico, the Republic of Texas, the United States military, and the state of Texas.

If Reed rode for the Rangers, he would have been a member of the Frontier Battalion, six companies of Rangers established in 1874 for the purpose of protecting settlers from the Indians and keeping peace on the frontier. By 1881, however, the Indian threat was over and the frontier was gone. Between 1886 and 1901, the Rangers kept busy taking care of railroad labor disputes, dealing with fence cutters and cattle rustlers, and troubleshooting for local law enforcement officials.

Reed often impressed his children and others about his life with the Rangers. One story that captivated his children dealt with his single-handed defense of a prisoner in his custody. Reed said that vigilantes – fourteen in all – were trying to impose their own brand of frontier justice on the prisoner. Reed stood his ground, and when the dust cleared only Reed and his captive were left standing. In his later years, Reed would recite a poem about the incident for his children. Most of the verses have been long forgotten, but his youngest daughter Ruth can still recall the last few lines:

So now he's free and ramblin'
And crowd him if you will
He's a Texas champion pistol shot
and they call him "Fearless Bill."

In other stories Reed recalled, he arrested horse thieves and cattle rustlers all over the state of Texas, using his tracking skills and ingenuity to bring in the guilty. He also had his fair share of shoot-outs with any man willing to call him out.

It is difficult to prove if William Reed was a Texas Ranger, as no one knows the alias he chose for himself at that time. While the rolls of the Frontier Battalion feature several men named William Reed, none match the man who came to be known as Deadshot. Reed was also skillful at telling his stories with as little detail as possible. He never revealed where or when the incidents he recalled took place, making it impossible to check out his stories.

According to Reed, it was during this time with the Rangers that he honed his shooting skills, working mostly with a Colt .45, a gun given to him by his father, one he carried his entire life. Reed practiced endlessly with this gun, until he could outdraw anyone with either hand. He was also adept at hiding it under his coat or arm, pointing it at people without their knowledge. In his early years, he used this skill to defend himself, but later this talent with a gun led to a long-term relationship with the Union Metallic Cartridge Company and Remington Steel, the nation's leading manufacturer of ammunition.

Following his service with the Texas Rangers, perhaps ending in the early 1890s, Reed told his children that he went to work for UMC. Hired because of his reputation with firearms, he became a performer in the company's shooting exhibitions, traveling all over the United States and abroad. While Reed was consistent in telling people he worked for UMC, his exploits more closely mirror those of Buffalo Bill's Wild West Show.

Buffalo Bill Cody, the founder of the original Wild West Show, established his traveling company in 1883 in Omaha, Nebraska. Cody, a buffalo hunter turned master showman, began producing melodramas about frontier life as early as 1873. The lure of the West made these so successful that Cody expanded the show in 1878 using real Indians. By 1883, he had a full-scale production company and drew such performers as Annie Oakley and Wild Bill Hickock. The show featured horse races, Indian battle re-enactments, buffalo hunts, and train robberies, all supposedly authentic and representing life in the "wild" west. The show also featured special performers who were excellent marksmen and horsemen.

Cody's exhibition was so well received that in 1887 the entire company traveled to England to take part in Queen Victoria's

Golden Jubilee; the company later returned to Europe in 1889 for a tour of the continent. In 1893 in Chicago, the troupe performed at the "World's Columbian Exposition," the World's Fair, where it drew large crowds. Buffalo Bill and his exploits would have been known to every boy in the United States.

UMC never had such an elaborate production. It simply took expert marksmen on tour, allowing these shooters to show off the company's ammunition. Oakley toured with UMC after she left Cody's Wild West Show in 1901, putting on free exhibitions throughout the country, but primarily in the East and Midwest.

Reed told his children that with UMC, he toured the United States and performed at the World's Fair in Chicago. He also said that he had performed before the queen of England and toured seven European countries. It was in Europe that he developed a dislike for arrogant people, especially Germans, whom he described as "uppity." In addition to his European travels, he said he was in China in 1900, stuck on a ship in a harbor near Peking (now Beijing) during the Boxer Rebellion, a short-lived uprising by a religious society attempting to expel foreigners from China. The uprising failed, and whether or not Reed and the UMC Wild West Show ever performed in China is unclear.

While Reed's travels may not be true, his relationship with UMC/Remington Steel seems valid. His children remember packages of guns and ammunition arriving at their home on the South Fork of the Salmon River, well into the 1920s. Pat Reed, Deadshot's son, remembered his father shooting targets and hunting with the ammunition, pistols, and rifles, all sent factory direct from Remington. Each spring Deadshot would go to Cascade and return with a package sent by the cartridge company. He would then set up targets and try out the different ammunition. As part of the arrangement, Reed, with his wife's help, would diligently record the results and then send a report back to Remington.

It was during his days with UMC, Reed told his family, that he picked up the name "Deadshot," a name he carried with pride. His ability to shoot quickly and accurately was well-known. He accepted any shooting challenge and was always ready to show off his prowess with a gun, even in his later years. According to one family story, Reed gave the citizens of Murphy, Idaho, a treat by shooting the perfect silhouette of an Indian onto a flat piece of tin. Reed did the handiwork in the 1930s, and the work hung in a Murphy establishment for several years.

Following Reed's tours with the wild west show, he went to work for UMC as a hunter and trapper. They sent him to Canada where he collected skins and heads to be mounted in the company's corporate headquarters. His wanderings took him to Harpers Camp, northern British Columbia, a mining community known for its lakes and streams. The area must have made a good impression on Reed, as he returned there later in his life.

After Harpers Camp, Reed apparently severed ties with UMC and headed north to the Yukon and Alaska. In the early 1900s, the Klondike goldrush had run its course, but many young men still sought their fortunes in the rugged area. Reed turned to card-playing as his livelihood. According to his daughter Ruth, it was in Alaska where Reed learned to stack and mark a deck of cards. He also learned to deal from the bottom of the deck. He often tried to impress his children with his card tricks, but most of the time he just made them angry. According to his daughter Anne, when it came to a game of cards, Reed never let his children win.

It was also during his Alaskan days that Reed began carrying a small silver derringer. He would wear it in his sleeve and was adept at moving it from his sleeve to his hand without anyone noticing. He often carried it, along with the Colt .45, hidden under his coat.

Reed's stay in Alaska was brief; he returned to San Antonio, Texas, where he met up with a young man who went by the name of George Moore—a younger brother or, perhaps, a half-brother. The two packed their meager belongings, said good-bye to Texas, and joined a cattle drive heading north to Idaho. This would lead to a new life and more drama than William Reed could ever imagine.

2

The Promise of Pierce

Hidden in the Clearwater region of north central Idaho, Pierce today is a sleepy little town, a far cry from its rough and tumble beginnings.

Pierce is the oldest mining community in Idaho, established in 1860 after the discovery of gold at Canal Gulch on Orofino Creek. The strike was made by a group of fortune seekers who had ignored government warnings about prospecting on Nez Perce Indian land. Led by Elias Davidson Pierce, the group made its initial strike in October, and over the next few months, the men staked claims, built shelter, and laid out the townsite for Pierce City. When miners poured into the area in the spring of 1861, Pierce became one of Idaho's first towns. Other communities soon followed, including Lewiston, which would become the hub of activity for northern Idaho.

Originally part of Washington Territory and Shoshone County, Pierce became the county seat in 1861. When Territorial elections were held later that year, more votes were cast in Shoshone County than any other part of the territory. Territorial officials in Olympia worried that the sudden shift in population to the gold fields of Idaho would mean a transfer in power, so they urged the formation of a new territory. The squabbling over boundaries lasted two years, but on March 4, 1863, Idaho Territory was established.

By the time Idaho became a territory, Pierce's gold fortunes had come and gone, with miners heading south for richer strikes in the Salmon River/Buffalo Hump and the Boise Basin/Idaho City areas. By 1869, only 100 men remained in the mining town. Chinese miners arrived in the late 1860s, and for the next thirty years, they comprised most of the population. The town suffered an even bigger setback in December of 1884 when the county seat was moved north to Murray, heart of the Coeur d' Alene mining activity.

Pierce refused to die, however. Some men turned to farming, raising cattle, horses, hay, and grain on the Weippe Prairie. They sold their products to the few remaining miners and to railroad crews who moved into the area in the late 1890s to extend the Northern Pacific Railway up the Clearwater River from Lewiston. The tracks at that time ended at Orofino, which became the center of commerce at the turn of the century.

Pierce benefited and in the early 1900s the town went through a revival. In 1902 a wagon road was built between Pierce and Orofino. Mining activity returned with the installation of a dredge on Orofino Creek. The timber industry, which eventually replaced mining, began in 1903 when the government opened the area for logging. The town boasted a post office, a grocery store, a drug store, a meat market, a barber shop, two blacksmith shops, two hotels, three livery stables, and three saloons.

Among those taking part in the boom were Aaron S. Warren and his wife Mary, who arrived in Pierce in the spring of 1896 along with their two children, Bessie and Willie. They would be joined ten years later by William Reed. His presence would cause both heartbreak and scandal for Pierce and the Warrens.

Aaron Warren was born in 1846 in Hopkinton, Massachusetts, a descendent of Richard Warren, a Pilgrim who had arrived in America on the Mayflower. Aaron's father, William, was a successful entrepreneur who ran a freight line, along with a dairy farm and a hotel. As a young man, Aaron worked on his father's farm and in his later life, he used the knowledge he gained there to succeed.

In the spring of 1861, Aaron watched as the young men of Massachussetts marched off to defend their country and their honor in the Civil War. Although only fifteen, he was caught up in the fervor and on Sept. 2, 1861, enlisted with Company A of the Twenty-Second Infantry Regiment of the Massachusetts Volunteers where he served as a musician, most likely a drummer.

Warren lasted less than a year. On August 8, 1862, he was discharged at Harrison's Landing, Virginia. Military records indicate he was sent home because of "extreme youth and physical disability." Undaunted, Warren re-enlisted in January 1864, this time joining the ranks of Company D of the Fourth Massachusetts Cavalry. Here he rose through the ranks, starting as a private and ending his service as a sergeant.

On August 17, 1864, Warren fought in the Battle of Gainesville, where he was captured by Confederate soldiers. He survived the notorious Andersonville Prison, in south central Georgia, then was moved to Florence, South Carolina. In February 1865, he won his freedom in a prisoner exchange and returned to his regiment. The next month, he was sent to the hospital for a three week stay, where he was treated for syphillis. He then returned to his unit and was mustered out in Richmond, Virginia, in November 1865.

Following the war, Warren followed thousands of others in the great western migration. He joined a 120-wagon train that trailed through Minnesota and into Helena, Montana, arriving there in 1866. He settled in Confederate Gulch and worked several mining claims. He also operated a profitable butchering business. His success would encourage further ventures in the cattle trade.

In 1871, Warren left Montana for California. There he established a contract with the Southern Pacific Railroad, supplying beef to the railroad crews who were laying tracks in a frenzied pace across the West. It was also during this time that he met his first wife, Mary Jones. They were married in San Francisco in 1873 and then moved to Virginia City, Nevada, where Warren and his two brothers opened a successful butcher shop.

Mary Jones Warren died in 1878. Soon after, for unknown reasons, Aaron Warren pulled up stakes and traveled to Idaho, settling first in the cattle and mining areas of Lemhi County. From there, he made his way to northern Idaho where he joined with two partners and put together a beef contract for the Northern Pacific Railroad, which was building lines throughout the area.

While Warren was supplying the railroad workers, businessman Thomas Kirby was trying to start a new community, Latah, thirty miles southeast of Lewiston. He struck a deal with the Northern Pacific to extend its line to the fledgling town. In return, Kirby built a wagon road into Latah and gave the railroad a deed to half of the township, 240 acres in all. He renamed the town Kendrick, in honor of the Northern Pacific's chief engineer. It was here Aaron Warren settled in the early 1890s.

Warren was one of the first business owners in Kendrick, opening a meat market there on Main Street in 1891. He also purchased several city lots, upon which he built his home. To supply his butcher shop, he ran cattle on the prairies north and east of Kendrick. He also became involved in Kendrick politics, serving as the community's second mayor.

Also arriving in Kendrick in the early 1890s was Mary R. Hutchinson. A Canadian from Prince Edward Island, Hutchinson arrived alone in Kendrick where she set up a hotel and dressmaker's shop. In her mid-twenties, her life prior to Kendrick is shadowy. At fourteen, she went to Boston to learn dressmaking and tailoring skills. On a return trip west to visit her family, she learned of Kendrick and decided to settle there, establishing her businesses in 1893. Hutchinson was extremely vague about her life prior to her move to Kendrick, saying only that she had married and had a daughter, Emily Grace, whom she left in the east with relatives. In reality, Emily Grace Hutchinson was born December 19, 1892, on Prince Edward Island, B.C. There she was raised by her grandmother, Elizabeth Hutchinson. Newspaper records show that Emily visited her mother at least once in Idaho, in 1907, and moved to Pierce at that time.

Bessie Warren

In Kendrick, Aaron Warren and Mary Hutchinson met, and inspite of their twenty-two year age difference, a romance soon followed. They were married on April 22, 1894, with their first child, Bessie Louise, born in February of 1895. A second child, George William (Willie) followed, although there is some discrepancy as to his date of birth. The 1900 census indicates that

Willie was born in October, 1897; Aaron Warren, when applying for his initial veteran's pension stated Willie was born Aug. 11, 1896; however, Willie's military records and death certificate indicate he was born August 12, 1895, in Kendrick. This inconsistency cannot be explained. However, Willie was born prior to the spring of 1896 because at that time, the Warrens sold all their possessions in Kendrick and moved to Pierce. Family records indicate Bessie and Willie were with their parents when they made the move.

It is unclear why the Warrens would give up their hotel and butcher business in a thriving Kendrick to move to Pierce, a town whose glory days were gone. Perhaps it was so Mary could be closer to her sister, Flora, who lived there with her blacksmith husband, John Richardson. It may have been because Aaron liked the cattle range on Quartz Creek, north of Pierce, or that he saw promise in several undeveloped mining claims there. Whatever the case, the Warrens built a substantial ranch on Quartz Creek, had another child Homer H. (Harry), and began making a new life for themselves.

While Mary busied herself raising the children and taking care of the home, Aaron expanded his business opportunities and became involved in the civic affairs of Pierce. In 1897 he was elected recorder for the Pierce mining district; he was also elected to the school board, a position he held for several years. He invested in both mining and land interests, expanded his cattle business, and established himself as a successful businessman.

The Warrens remained on Quartz Creek until 1901. Then, with Bessie ready to start school, the family began looking for lodging in Pierce. They bought the City Hotel on Main Street which served as both the family home and a business venture. The hotel had nineteen rooms, and Mary kept busy maintaining the rooms and serving meals in the large dining room on the main

Aaron and Mary Warren with their children, Bessie, Willie, and Harry

floor. Aaron continued to operate the ranch on Quartz Creek and also established a livery and feed barn on the edge of town to work in conjunction with the hotel. He ran a weekly advertisement in the *Pierce City Miner* which read "Reasonable rates made for board and lodging by day or week. When you are hungry, then remember the City Hotel. Feed stables in connection."

In the beginning the hotel was successful, and Mary became well-known around the community for her hospitality. She was left to do the bulk of the hotel work as Aaron continued his mining and ranching activities on Quartz Creek. According to information in the *Pierce City Miner* throughout 1902 and 1903, he was out of town much of the time, delivering cattle, getting in hay, butchering stock, or filing new mining claims. In his absence, Mary turned to the children, especially Bessie, for help around the hotel. Before she went to school each morning, Bessie was responsible for changing the guest beds and setting the tables in the dining room. At night she helped serve dinner to the guests then cleared the tables when they were through. Later in her life Bessie remembered the work as exhausting and her mother as demanding. Mary Warren expected Bessie, only eight years old, to work as hard as an adult. Still Bessie benefited from it. From her mother's example, she learned the value of hard work and how to be a gracious hostess. She also learned to cook, mend, sew, and preserve fruits, vegetables, and meat, all under the critical eye of Mary.

Perhaps Aaron appreciated Mary's hard work—managing the hotel and raising the children—for in September of 1902, he advertised the City Hotel was for rent. Then in October the couple left for a two week vacation to visit the Spokane and Lewiston fairs. Aaron explained to the local paper that the getaway was their "wedding trip." The couple also did some shopping while they were gone. They returned to Pierce with a new ten-burner Majestic Range with a sixty pound broiler. Aaron installed it in the hotel and began running a new advertisement in the newspaper: "City Hotel. Best Tables in the Pierce District. Sunday Chicken Dinners. Good Warm Rooms."

The hotel's success, however, was overshadowed by the Pioneer Hotel, located directly across the street. The Pioneer was the site of many Pierce civic activities, including town meetings and dances. The newspaper even ran lists of guests who stayed at the Pioneer, most of them well-known throughout the social and business circles of northern Idaho. Not glamorous like the Pioneer, the City Hotel served transient miners and cattlemen who passed through Pierce. They kept the Warrens in business.

The family also benefited financially from Aaron's Civil War service. In March 1903, he applied for an invalid pension, stating he suffered from rheumatism, piles, and cramps in his limbs. He also claimed he was deaf in one ear. A doctor confirmed his physical ailments, and Aaron was given a pension of six dollars per month for partial disability. Over the next several years, Aaron would reapply for increased benefits. In January 1905, Aaron traveled to Lewiston for a medical checkup. A doctor there diagnosed Aaron with diseases of the heart and rectum, along with the rheumatism and deafness. He had also lost the vision in his right eye. His pension would be increased to eight dollars a month. Eventually, this sum would be raised to twelve dollars a month.

Even with his disabilities, Aaron continued to take care of the ranch. For her part, Mary ran the hotel, but she was rarely mentioned in the local section of the paper. Aaron's activities, however, were well-noted. Then in September of 1906, the couple had a fourth child, a girl, whom they named Gladys Irene. She would be called Irene.

It was shortly after the birth of Irene that the Warrens began having problems, although Bessie Warren would later relate that her parents' relationship was never a happy one. According to Bessie, Aaron Warren was an alcoholic; he often forced her to go out and buy him whiskey when he was too drunk to do so. Mary Warren put up with him, mainly for the sake of the children, but by 1907 she wanted out of the marriage. She continued to provide for the family by running the hotel, but information in the Pierce newspaper indicates she was also branching out on her own.

In February 1907, the *Miner* reported that Mary, by herself, attended a dance given by the I.O.O.F. What is interesting to note here is that for the first time she was referred to as "Mary"

Warren. All preceding references to her had addressed her as "Mrs. A.S. Warren." In April of the same year, Mary purchased a building from the town's shoemaker and had it razed. While it is unknown what she did with the property, it is clear she was acting independently of Aaron.

Throughout the summer of 1907, Mary Warren made trips to Lewiston, sometimes accompanied by her children, Harry and Bessie, but often alone. Then in November, Mary's mother, Elizabeth Hutchinson, arrived for a visit, accompanied by Mary's daughter Emily. When Elizabeth left Pierce, Emily remained. Her stay must have put additional strain on the Warrens' disintegrating relationship. Then in July of 1908, Elizabeth returned for a visit, staying with Mary at the hotel. Her visit gave her daughter the moral support she needed, for on July 24, 1908, Mary traveled to Lewiston where she filed for a divorce, accusing Aaron of cruel and inhuman treatment and failure to provide.

Another factor also figured into the breakup of Aaron and Mary Warren—William Reed. It is unclear whether he hurried the breakup along, but it is certain that Reed and Mary knew each other as early as 1907, possibly before. Through the spring and summer of 1908, he was a frequent guest at the City Hotel where he was friendly with Mary and her children. Mary must have appreciated the attention of the handsome Texas cowboy who carried himself with extraordinary self-confidence. With Aaron gone much of the time and abusive when he was home, Reed must have seemed a welcome relief. By fall of 1908, it would become apparent that Mary Warren and William Reed were more than just acquaintances.

3

Cattle Rustling

Although court records indicate William Reed was in the Pierce area as early as 1905, it was not until June 1907 that his name earned mention in the *Pierce City Miner*. The paper reported that Reed was living in Summit, seven miles north of Pierce, and was taking 100 head of cattle to Breakfast Creek, also north of Pierce, to range for the season. On his trips into town throughout the summer, he lodged at the City Hotel. He became a recognized face in Pierce, setting up accounts at T.B. Reed's mercantile and the local slaughterhouse.

Reed worked with A.J. Sloan and Arthur (Chester) Rice, two other cattlemen in the area. Along with Reed was a young man named George Moore. While he is never mentioned with Reed in Pierce, Moore was apparently Reed's younger brother, born in Texas in 1882. In court records, Reed referred to Moore as his partner and called him "Kid." In his later years, Reed made it clear to his family that Moore was his brother. Throughout the summers of 1907 and 1908, the four men would herd and butcher cows around Pierce and Orofino, selling their beef to the local meat markets or hiring themselves out to cattlemen to take care of their herds.

Herding cattle on the prairies around Pierce was a challenging proposition. Open range caused cattle from various sources to mix, making it difficult to keep track of ownership. Many ranchers would just turn their stock loose in the spring and not look for them until fall. Strays would wander from one herd to the next, and it was not unusual that a single herd might contain the brands of many different cattle owners. Added to this was the stock from the Nez Perce, which often was not branded, and cattle whose brands had been altered. If a brand was altered with a running iron, it was impossible to be sure of the real brand until the cow was dead and the inside of the hide could be examined.

Accusations of cattle rustling were common but usually resolved peacefully. Such was the case in the fall of 1905 when Reed and Moore sold a steer in Orofino, only to have A.D. (Dan) Carr claim it was not theirs to sell. Carr, who had ranched in the Orofino area since 1898, confronted Reed about the steer. While Reed never admitted stealing the animal, he returned it to Carr, and the matter was dropped. Although the two men would later say they harbored no hard feelings, it was clear they had not completely buried the hatchet. The problems between the two men would resurface and lead to a real wild west shoot-out.

In July of 1908, Reed was hired by the First National Bank of Pullman, Washington. His charge was to gather the cattle of the Ringer estate near Pierce on which the bank held a mortgage. When Reed collected the cattle, he found the brands had been altered, with the new brand made to look like that of A.D. Carr. It is unknown why Reed did not go to the authorities with this information. Instead, he and his partners herded the cattle to Quartz Creek. Moore and Sloan stayed with the cattle on Quartz Creek, while Reed and Rice took seven head to Pierce where they butchered them in the local slaughterhouse. This took place Monday afternoon, July 27, 1908. Finishing their task, both Reed and Rice rented rooms at the City Hotel.

That evening Ben Craig of Pierce rode to the Carr Ranch, six miles east of Orofino, to tell his uncle, A.D. Carr, that Reed had butchered some of his cattle. Carr dispatched his two oldest boys, Albert and Homer, to check out the situation. They rode into

Pierce early the next morning and investigated the slaughterhouse. Their way was barred, but they were able to discern several carcasses hanging in the slaughterhouse. Homer stayed to guard the slaughterhouse while Albert made the half-mile ride into Pierce City to look for Reed.

He did not have to look far as he headed straight to the City Hotel where he found Rice and Reed. On the street in front of the hotel, Albert confronted Reed. According to Albert, Reed stalled for time, while Rice, on Reed's instructions, headed to the slaughterhouse to get away with the hide of one particular cow. When Rice returned to tell Reed that someone was guarding the slaughterhouse, Reed told Albert he did not want any trouble, and he was willing to "compromise." The two men then made their way to the slaughterhouse where they examined the hide.

Homer Carr picked up the hide and showed Reed the Carr brand, a connected 76. Reed seemed unimpressed and sent Rice to find the livery man Emmet Barrows. Reed wanted Barrows to haul the beef to the butcher shop in Pierce. When Barrows arrived and attempted to remove the carcass, the Carrs objected. Albert wanted his father to examine the scene before any evidence was removed.

Court records indicate discrepancies as to what happened next, but according to Barrows, Reed asked the Carr brothers if they had a warrant. When they could not produce one, Reed pulled his Colt .45 and told the Carrs to get in a line. He told the brothers they could have the hide, but they could not have the beef because it was his to sell. After several anxious exchanges, the boys relented. Barrows then hauled the beef to the Salings Butcher Shop in Pierce.

The confrontation had been tense. According to Albert's court testimony, Reed was livid when the Carrs told him he could not take the meat to the butcher.

"I would just as soon kill you than to take dictation from you," Reed told Albert. "Not you or any other son of a bitch can dictate what I can do with the carcass of this animal."

Reed also acknowledged that the butchered steer might get him into trouble, but he was not willing to submit to the Carrs. He must have felt that threatening the Carrs was the best way out of the situation. According to Barrows, Reed admitted that he could be in for some jail time.

"If it is your animal, I will probably get six years for killing it," Reed said while holding the Carrs at gunpoint. Albert Carr said Reed added to this statement "and I might as well get ninety-nine. I'll kill you both with one shot."

Once the carcass was gone, the scene was over. The Carrs took the hide in question, leaving the others, and then headed to the Pierce livery stable where they fed their horses. They took an empty feed sack from the livery and put the hide in it. Then they headed home to face their father. For their part, Reed and Rice rode out of Pierce, probably to Quartz Creek, to inform Sloan and Moore what had transpired.

Upon returning to the Carr Ranch, Albert and Homer explained to their father the events of that morning. Daniel Carr decided it was time to let the law handle the case. He took the hide and rode into Orofino, where he swore out a complaint against Reed, Sloan, Moore, and Rice, charging them with grand larceny for the theft of a two-year-old, red and white cow.

Newspapers report that both Sloan and Rice appeared in Orofino on July 31 to answer the charge, where Rice was held over, but Sloan was released on a $100 bond. When Moore and Reed failed to appear, Orofino Constable Miles (Matt) Cochran, armed with a warrant, traveled to Pierce to find them but was unsuccessful. Then on Sunday evening, Reed rode into Orofino where he gave himself up to the constable. Cochran officially arrested Reed but saw no need to lock him up, trusting Reed would show up at his preliminary hearing the next morning.

In 1908 Orofino was part of Nez Perce County. While each community in the county had its own constable and justice of the peace, major legal proceedings in the county were dictated by prosecuting attorneys dispatched from Lewiston, the county seat. In the larceny matter against Reed and Rice, county attorney Daniel Needham was called in to prosecute the case.

Needham arrived in Orofino early Monday morning to gather information. He met with Daniel Carr, his wife Phoebe, and his sons Albert, Homer, and Gordon, along with Ben Craig. They brought with them the hide taken from the Pierce slaughterhouse, along with other pieces of hide that Craig had collected. He also met with Constable Cochran and several others in the community. Once his preliminary investigation was over, Needham realized that Reed and Rice had too many friends and sympathizers in Orofino; no jury would convict them. Thus, at the start of the preliminary hearing, Needham rose before Orofino Justice of the Peace John Chandler and moved for a change of venue. Chandler denied the motion. Then, using his power as prosecuting attorney, Needham moved to dismiss the case against the two men, which was granted. He then ordered them re-arrested, with the intent of bringing new charges against them. These charges would be heard in a Lewiston courtroom. When the proceeding was over, Needham explained himself to the Carrs, assuring them this was the best way to bring the cattle thieves to justice. The Carrs, still in possession of the hide, left Orofino bound for their ranch. Ben Craig also went with them.

Rice and Reed were alarmed with the sudden turn of events. Constable Cochran would later relate that both men were "surprised and distressed about the transfer of the case to Lewiston." Sensing their anxiety, Needham told Cochran to hire extra men to assist him in getting Reed and Rice to Lewiston, but Cochran did not see the need. Instead, he told the two men to get something to eat. In the meantime, he would make travel arrangements for the three of them to make the trip by train to Lewiston later that afternoon. Cochran then returned to his own home to have his mid-day meal.

Discrepancies exist as to what happened next, but Reed and Rice had no intention of traveling to Lewiston for a trial in front of a hostile prosecuting attorney and an unknown jury. First, they had a brief conversation with a lawyer, I.N. Smith, of Orofino. Rice and Reed then split up. Reed visited a bank where he tried to withdraw $500, only to be denied. Following this, he went to Cochran's house, indicating he would go with the constable to the train station. Rice was to meet them there. On the way, Reed asked to stop at the home of J.W. Scott, who owned the livery stable. Reed went into the house, while Cochran and Scott talked outside. When Reed reappeared, he was carrying a Winchester rifle belonging to Scott. He calmly walked by the two men, mounted his horse, and bade them good-bye. He rode away, quickly meeting up with Rice, also on horseback. On the outskirts of Orofino, they were joined by Sloan and Moore. Together the four men made their getaway.

Constable Cochran, unarmed and overwhelmed, immediately sought the assistance of prosecuting attorney Needham, but Needham was nowhere to be found. Knowing he would have hell to pay, Cochran found a pistol, borrowed a horse, and went after the four outlaws. He would fire one or two shots at the group, only to have them return fire. Knowing he was outnumbered and outgunned, he returned to Orofino where he hoped to gather a posse but found no volunteers. Eventually he found Needham and informed him of the escape.

If there is a villain in what transpired next, it may have been Needham. Upon hearing of the escape, Needham phoned all

Main Street, Orofino, in 1910 (Idaho State Historical Society Photo)

the ranches along the Orofino-Pierce road in search of the Carrs. Perhaps he thought it was necessary to warn them of the fugitives, thinking Reed and his companions would harm them. Perhaps he thought the rustlers would attempt to steal the cow hide, the only real evidence against them. Whatever the case, before the Carrs reached home, they knew the outlaws had escaped, and they were on the alert. In fact, according to Daniel Carr, Needham had deputized the Carrs and Craig, with orders to bring the outlaws back "dead or alive." They planned to do just that.

But the Carrs were not heavily armed. Among them, they had just three revolvers, certainly not enough to fight off a desperate pack of rustlers. Daniel saw the need for more fire power, so he stopped at the ranch of Archie Bonner, a relative, and borrowed a rifle, which he placed underneath the seat of his buggy. Then they continued east. At the Payne Snyder cabin, one mile west of the Carr ranch, they set up an ambush. Homer, Albert, and Ben Craig hid their horses and lay in wait. For safety, Daniel and Phoebe continued toward their ranch with young Gordon on horseback following.

Daniel and Phoebe had traveled only about a mile before they heard shots and knew their sons and nephew were in a fight with Reed and his partners. They pulled up at a place known as Carr Springs, a watering trough, where Dan left the buggy in the hands of Phoebe. He took the rifle and hid himself in some thick brush, approximately forty feet north of the trough. Also at the trough were Frank, Olive, and Clara Altendeder, brother and sisters, who just happened to be passing by. They would witness some of the action.

The Altendeders talked briefly to Phoebe and Gordon Carr, enough to learn that cattle rustlers had escaped from Orofino and one of them, a man named Reed, "was an expert with a gun." Phoebe and Gordon then continued east toward the Carr Ranch. The Altendeders followed.

No one was at the spring when Reed, Sloan, Rice, and Moore arrived. Sloan and Moore reached the trough first, followed by Rice. Reed trailed the group by about fifteen yards. When Reed pulled his horse up to get a drink, Dan Carr shot, hitting Reed in the right arm and knocking his rifle out of his hand. Reed's horse spooked and reared-back, while Moore's horse, on Reed's right, pitched forward. Sloan's horse also bolted. Carr shot twice more, this time hitting Moore and Sloan. They ended up 100 yards east of the trough before they could get their horses stopped.

Reed, his right arm badly damaged, dismounted and retrieved his rifle. He made his way up an embankment hoping to get a clear look at the shooter. Shortly, Carr emerged from the brush, his rifle at the ready. He saw Reed, but before he could get off another shot, Reed fired. Carr took off running to the east. Reed took aim again, knocking Carr down with his second shot. Carr got up, only to have Reed shoot him again. Reed fired once more, hitting Carr for the third time. At this point, Reed was overcome with his own injuries. For the next few minutes he lay in a heap at the bottom of the embankment. Rice, who had taken cover at the start of the shooting, went to Reed's aid. Together they made their way to check on Sloan and Moore.

Sloan was sitting in the middle of the road, an ugly but non-threatening flesh wound on his neck. Beside him, Moore lay mortally wounded, a bullet lodged in his back between his left hip and spine. Nothing could be done for him, and he died shortly after Reed reached him. Reed rolled his brother over to take a look at the wound. The bullet had passed through a leather money belt Moore had been wearing. Over the course of the next several months, Reed and Rice told various stories concerning the money belt, although Reed would later tell his family that he took the money and the belt, which he kept for the rest of his life. Later newspaper reports would state that Moore had been carrying over $1,400, money the group had intended to use for bail in the cattle rustling charge.

The fugitives had little time to discuss their next move. The Carr brothers were sure to arrive on the scene at any moment, and once they found their father, they would want revenge.

The three fugitives mounted their horses and headed east. At some point, Sloan went ahead of the group while Rice stayed with the injured Reed. Rice and Reed headed northeast to a place known as Carr Lake, about 1 1/2 miles from the watering trough. Reed was badly injured and could go no further. Rice helped him from his horse and stayed with him for a short time, but he was convinced Reed's wound was fatal. When Reed lost consciousness, Rice left. He joined Sloan, and the two made their way to Rice's cabin, eight miles northeast of Orofino.

About the same time, the Carr brothers discovered their father lying in the brush about forty yards from the watering trough. All four of Reed's shots had struck the elder Carr, but none of the wounds were life threatening. The boys carried their father to the home of Archie Bonner, where he received initial medical treatment. He would later be taken to a hospital in Moscow, Idaho, where he would recover from his wounds.

News of the shootout reached Orofino almost immediately. Constable Cochran notified Needham in Lewiston, who then contacted the Nez Perce County Deputy Sheriff Ab Masters. Masters instructed Cochran to gather men from Orofino, Weippe, and Pierce to search for the fugitives. However, Cochran was unable to muster a posse out of Pierce, as Reed and his partners were well-known and respected there. An article in the Pierce City Miner immediately following the shoot-out called Reed and Moore "quiet and inoffensive men." Many residents of Pierce, including Mary Warren, would come to Reed's aid in the weeks and months following the shooting.

Cochran led his Orofino posse to the Carr Ranch. There they retrieved the body of Moore but were unable to locate Reed, Rice, and Sloan. Cochran returned to Orofino that evening to await further instructions from Masters.

Masters arrived on Tuesday morning to take over the search. While he was in hot pursuit of the fugitives, prosecuting attorney Needham, along with county coroner Vassar held an inquest concerning the death of George Moore. Needham and Vassar called four witnesses: Dr. Fairley, Albert Carr, Ben Craig, and Archie Bonner. Fairley described the nature of Moore's fatal gunshot wound. Carr, Craig, and Bonner described the fray, laying the blame for the entire affair on the escaped cattle rustlers. None of the witnesses implicated Dan Carr in the shooting, and he was never called to testify, although he was in the courtroom during the inquest. Following the testimony, the jury of six men concluded that Moore died from a gunshot wound fired by a party or parties unknown and that George Moore "was one of four parties who first opened fire." With that, Needham and the coroner returned to Lewiston, and Dan Carr made his way to the hospital in Moscow. Later that afternoon, Moore was buried in the Orofino cemetery.

Reed and his partners were unaware of the events in Orofino. Reed was by himself and near death beside Carr Lake. Rice and Sloan were hiding out in familiar territory northeast of the town. The two managed to elude capture on Tuesday, but on Wednesday afternoon, Masters and his posse began closing in on Rice's cabin, where Rice and Sloan had been lying low. When they left the cabin on foot, they were confronted by Masters and deputy Andrew Shaw. Seeing it was the law, and not the Carrs, Rice and Sloan surrendered.

They were arrested and taken to Orofino. On the way, they related the details of the shooting from their perspective. Rice also informed Masters that he had left Reed at Carr Lake in bad shape. Masters then contacted Bill Castor and Robert Cooper, two friends of Reed who lived in the vicinity. They went in search of Reed and found him Wednesday evening. Hungry, bloody, his shattered arm showing the first signs of infection, Reed was ready to give up. Masters was contacted, and in the early morning hours of August 6, Masters delivered Reed to the Orofino jail.

The next day, Reed, Rice, and Sloan were transferred to Lewiston by train. Rice and Sloan were immediately placed in the Nez Perce County jail while Reed was taken to St. Joseph's Hospital where doctors endeavored to repair his arm. For his part, prosecuting attorney Needham began legal maneuverings that would consume all parties involved for the next nine months.

4

Trials and Troubles

It is important to note that through Reed's entire ordeal—the escape from Orofino, the shoot-out, the eventual capture—he was actually a free man. When he originally appeared before the Orofino Justice of the Peace, the charges of cattle rustling against him had been dismissed, at the request of prosecuting attorney Needham. While Needham intended to refile charges against him, at the time Reed rode away from Orofino on August 3, no warrants were held for his arrest. Needham must have realized this oversight, for by the time Reed arrived at St. Joseph's Hospital in Lewiston, Needham had refiled grand larceny charges against Reed. However, proceedings would be put on hold until both Reed and Dan Carr recovered from their wounds.

Reed was in desperate physical condition, his right arm critically damaged. Struck in the forearm, he suffered a fracture at the point of impact, with the bone splintered and damaged beyond repair. The exit wound left a gaping hole. Doctors at first advised Reed to give up his arm; they believed without the amputation, he would die from infection. But Reed resisted, asking the doctors to "take every chance." They respected his wishes, and, miraculously, the arm healed. While he never regained total strength or flexibility in his right arm or hand, he practiced so much with his left hand, particularly shooting, that few noticed his disability.

Reed remained hospitalized for at least three weeks following the incident. A report in the *Lewiston Morning Tribune* on

August 19 indicated he was still a patient at St. Joseph's, and Needham was impatiently waiting to set a preliminary trial date. In preparation for his trial, Reed hired Clay McNamee and Judge James Harn, well-known lawyers who would prove invaluable to his cause.

Reed's arraignment on the cattle rustling charge was called on August 27 before Judge Arthur Hazen in the District Court, Second Judicial District, Lewiston, Idaho. Testimony began on September 3, with Dan, Homer, and Albert Carr testifying, along with Emmet Barrows. Prosecuting attorney Needham, eager to get the trial against Reed underway, led the questioning with frequent objections from McNamee. Dan Carr also produced a hide and claimed it was the same one taken from Reed at the Pierce slaughterhouse on July 27. Once the testimony was over, Hazen found there was sufficient evidence to hold Reed for trial. He set an arraignment date for October 14 and fixed Reed's bail at $2,000.

Reed posted bond with the help of Mary Warren and then began some legal maneuvering of his own. He had his lawyers file charges against Dan Carr for the murder of Moore. They also filed assault charges against Carr, his sons, and Ben Craig.

Needham was furious. He had overseen the inquest of Moore. He had cleared the Carrs of all wrongdoing, believing instead that Reed and his band of outlaws were responsible for the entire shootout. After Reed, Rice, and Sloan were bound over on the cattle rustling charge, Needham filed an additional charge against them, this time assault with the intent to commit murder.

Legal wrangling continued throughout September with charges and counter charges. Later in the fall, the assault charges against Reed and his partners would be dropped, but Dan Carr would be held on the murder charge. After months of motions and delays, the trial of Dan Carr was set for April 26, 1909. In

The District Courthouse in Lewiston where William Reed's trial was held (Idaho State Historical Society Photo)

the meantime, Carr was released on $5,000 bond.

While Carr was attempting to delay his trial, Reed was doing his best to see that his case for grand larceny would also be postponed. Once out on bail, he spent time in Pierce, staying at the City Hotel, visiting with his friends, and lining up a defense. Mary Warren, who had traveled to Lewiston for Reed's preliminary hearing, was an attentive hostess, caring for his needs. In addition, Mary had information concerning strips of hide that Ben Craig had in his possession. Craig planned to turn them over to Needham to use against Reed at his trial. Mary became not only an important witness to Reed; she also became his confidante, his staunch supporter. While there is no clear proof of an affair between Reed and Mary Warren, it is clear that by

Reed's arraignment in October, the two had developed a very close relationship.

At the arraignment, Reed's lawyers asked for a continuance until October 17 in order for them to examine the evidence. The request was granted. On October 17, McNamee filed a motion to quash the physical evidence in the trial, the cow hide. McNamee argued there had been no chain of control over the hide. He contended there was no guarantee that the hide in evidence was the hide collected at the Pierce slaughterhouse. That motion was denied, and Reed entered a plea of "not guilty." The plea was accepted and the judge set a trial date for October 26. Reed once again returned to Pierce to await his day in court.

On October 26, he appeared in court where lawyer McNamee asked for a continuance. As part of Reed's defense, McNamee had subpoenaed several witnesses including George Englehorn (Engleholm). Englehorn had helped Reed butcher the alleged stolen beef, and McNamee claimed his testimony was crucial to Reed's defense. Englehorn would testify that the hide presented in evidence did not belong to the cow he and Reed butchered. However, Englehorn could not be found and the subpoena could not be served. Thus McNamee was asking for more time so Englehorn could be located. This request was granted and the trial was rescheduled.

When court convened on November 20, McNamee once again asked for a continuance, this time until the next term of the district court. Englehorn, his most important witness, still could not be located. Several witnesses, including deputy sheriff Masters, testified that Englehorn was trapping in the mountains northeast of Pierce and with the early snowfall in the mountains, it was futile to try to find him. The court agreed, and Reed's trial was postponed until the next court session. Reed, still out on bail, split time between Myrtle and Pierce for the next two months.

In late January 1909, Reed's case was called. McNamee once again issued subpoenas to witnesses, including Mary Warren and George Englehorn. They would testify as to the credibility of the state's evidence. This time, all the witnesses were available, and on February 9 the trial began.

Jury selection took two days. Once the jury was seated, Needham presented his evidence, calling to the stand Dan, Homer, and Albert Carr along with Ben Craig, Emmet Barrows, and M.L. Johnson. There were no surprises, as all men testified to the events of July 27, 1908, surrounding the Pierce slaughterhouse, the taking of the hide, and Reed's reactions. Then it was McNamee's turn.

McNamee examined Englehorn, who testified that the cow he and Reed had butchered on July 27 was branded with the figure "20" along with a triangle H. The hide presented as evidence carried the brand of Dan Carr, the linked 76. But McNamee's real ace in the hole was the testimony of two Nez Perce Indians. They claimed the hide brought to court actually came from a heifer belonging to them; they further claimed that Dan Carr had stolen the heifer and re-marked it with his brand.

McNamee also called several character witnesses, but it was the testimony of Englehorn and the Nez Perce that closed the deal. The jury found Reed not guilty of the grand larceny charge, and he was a free man. With the conclusion of his case, the charges against Rice and Sloan were also dropped.

Mary Warren was never called to testify in the case, although she attended the proceedings each day. Perhaps McNamee thought her relationship with Reed would taint her credibility, or perhaps he didn't need her. It is unclear whether anyone knew at the time that Mary was four months pregnant. When the trial was over, she remained in Lewiston for another week, and then returned to Pierce, where she was joined by Reed. He looked into purchasing the local butcher shop, and during the first week of March he became proprietor of the Pierce City Meat Market. He ran an advertisement in the *Pierce City Miner* that read "City Meat Market, W.P. Reed Proprietor, Fresh and Salt Meat, Game & Fish in Season at Prices that are Right."

There remained only one matter left to resolve concerning the cattle rustling incident, and that was the murder trial for Dan Carr. Jury selection began on April 26 and testimony was underway the next day. Working on the prosecution team were D.E. Hodge and Reed's lawyers McNamee and Harn, who offered their services to the state. Carr was represented by George W. Tannahill. Needham, who had done his best to put Reed in jail, would testify on behalf of Carr.

The trial took five days. The prosecution called thirteen witnesses, including Reed, Rice, and Sloan, and the Altendeders, who had witnessed some of the incident. The defense called twenty-four witnesses, ten of them related to the Carrs. Gordon Carr, the youngest son of Dan Carr was the key defense witness. Prior to the shoot-out, Gordon claimed he took a phone message from Needham. Needham told him to warn his father about the escape of Reed and his partners. Gordon also stated that Needham told him to tell his father to organize a posse and bring the outlaws back "dead or alive."

In his instructions, the judge advised the jury that a person has the right to kill in an effort to arrest parties charged with a felony. He also explained the self-defense law which allows a person to kill another in the attempt to protect himself. The jury paid close attention; they took less than two hours to acquit Carr of all charges.

Disappointed but not surprised, Reed returned to Pierce to run his butcher shop. While there would be no more trouble between Reed and his rivals, he would never forgive Dan Carr for killing his brother; forty years after the incident he would still tell his children, "Never trust a Carr."

5

Reed Wears Out His Welcome

With all the legal issues resolved, Reed turned his attention to making a living in Pierce. All indications are that he lived at the City Hotel and was a companion to Mary Warren. He also renewed his partnership with Sloan, as in mid-May 1909, they began running cattle near Pierce and on Quartz Creek. His name appeared frequently in the *Pierce City Miner*, and the advertisement for his butcher shop continued to run on a weekly basis.

For his part Aaron Warren busied himself at his ranch at Quartz Creek. In the summer of 1908, shortly after Mary had filed for divorce, he was joined by his brother, James H. Warren from Butte, Montana, who had arrived in Pierce in his private rail car. Bessie Warren would later describe her uncle as "well-to-do" and called his rail car a "palace on wheels." James's visit must have been helpful to Aaron as he began to suffer significant health problems. In December 1908, he traveled to Spokane where he had surgery to remove a cataract on his right eye; his recuperation there took over one month. He also was plagued by heart problems. In a request for an increase to his veteran's pension, Aaron submitted a letter from Dr. Elmore Frey of Pierce. Frey claimed that Aaron Warren was indeed worthy of an increase in pension because "he is liable to die at any time from heart trouble." Whether or not Aaron had turned to Mary to help him with his health problems is unclear.

As for Mary, once the cattle rustling trial was over, she returned to Pierce where she continued to run the City Hotel and await the birth of her child. In May, she ran a notice in the *Pierce City Miner*, advertising Wyandotte eggs and roosters for sale, but other than that, she stayed out of sight. Even the birth of her sixth child, Charles Frederick, on July 11, 1909, did not earn a mention in the local newspaper. This seems to substantiate the notion that this child was not Aaron's, and thus, not a celebration but a scandal.

If Charles Frederick was not Aaron Warren's child, but perhaps William Reed's, as some people conjectured, what happened next almost defies belief. On July 24, William Reed and Mary's daughter, Bessie Warren, secretly left Pierce. They traveled to Spokane where on July 28, 1909, they were married before a justice of the peace. In order to do so, however, Bessie had to lie about her age. A notice of their ceremony appeared in the July 29 edition of the *Spokesman Review*, a Spokane newspaper: "Licensed to Wed: William P. Reid (33) to Bernice L. Warren (18), both of Pierce, Idaho." The *Pierce City Miner* repeated the news on July 30, alerting the entire community to the event.

Mary Warren was devastated. She depended heavily on Bessie in the everyday affairs of the hotel and the family. Now Mary had to take care of guests and her children, including the new baby, without Bessie's able assistance. And if Mary had been in a relationship with Reed, surely the town gossips were having a good laugh at her expense. Mary had been duped and humiliated by the sweet talking, good-looking, manipulative Texan who had eloped with her fourteen-year-old daughter.

If Mary and Aaron were still estranged during the first half of 1909, Bessie's elopement brought them together. Aaron was infuriated that Reed had absconded with his daughter, and he began arrangements that would bring her home. But on August 2, Aaron suffered a paralyzing stroke and was hospitalized in

At 13, Bessie posed for a Lewiston photographer.

Lewiston. Mary left the children and the hotel in the care of others to be with Aaron. Clearly, her fortunes had suddenly changed, and she needed both the moral and financial support of her husband if she were to survive.

They remained in Lewiston for three weeks. Aaron was then sent to the Soldiers Home in Boise to continue recuperation; Mary returned to Pierce to run the hotel and take care of business at the ranch on Quartz Creek.

As for Bessie, she saw the marriage to Reed as a way to escape her unhappy life in Pierce. She would later tell her children that she sometimes felt like a slave working in the hotel, forced each day by her mother to change and wash bedding, set and clear tables, and help prepare meals for guests. She was also largely responsible for her younger brothers and sister, changing diapers and watching over them as her mother worked to keep the hotel in business. Bessie saw William Reed as a handsome, considerate, and adventurous man, who would bring her a better life, away from her demanding mother and drunken father. For Reed, the young, striking Bessie with her haunting blue eyes and dark hair was a good catch. He knew she could cook, sew, and keep house, and, unlike her mother, she had no commitments. To him, she would be the perfect wife.

At the end of August, Reed and his child bride returned briefly to Pierce, where they stayed at the Pioneer Hotel. Reed turned over his meat market to J.P. Partridge and then headed to the Musselshell District, southeast of Pierce, to check on his cattle interests. Bessie tried to make amends with her mother, but Mary Warren was too proud and too angry. Bessie collected a few of her treasured possessions—a crocheted doily, pictures of herself and her family, a piece of china. She also took her sewing machine, a black, foot-treadle Singer. Then she left Pierce and her family to begin her new life with Reed. She would not speak to her mother again for over twenty years.

Reed would have one final confrontation with Mary Warren. On Sept. 14, 1909, Mary filed a complaint against Reed with the District Court of Nez Perce County, alleging that on July 24, 1909, W.P. Reed "surreptitiously enticed and took away with him Bessie Warren, infant daughter of the plaintiff." Her complaint asserted that the couple had been married in Spokane, but because Bessie was only fourteen, not the legal age of consent, the marriage should be annulled.

Reed responded to the charges on October 2, claiming that Mary did not have any legal standing in the case, nor did she know the facts. He also maintained that the Nez Perce District Court had no jurisdiction in the matter, since the marriage took

Bessie, center, and William Reed, far right, near Pierce, shortly after their elopement

place in Spokane. Mary, in the courtroom with her attorney, realized Reed was not about to give up his new bride. Rather than prolong the scandal, Mary dropped the charges and returned to Pierce. Reed and Bessie settled in Myrtle, sixty-three miles west of Pierce, where Reed once again went to work herding cattle.

As for Mary, the next several years would be extremely difficult. Aaron returned from the veteran's hospital in late September, and Mary slowly nursed him back to health. Eventually he was able to return to his cattle and mining interests but never regained his full strength. He took on a hired hand and over the next two years, together they worked the herd at the Quartz Creek Ranch. Mary continued to operate the City Hotel and raise the children.

In the spring of 1911, Aaron applied for an increase to his $12 a month veteran's pension. In this application, he acknowledged Charles Frederick as his son. He also claimed that he was nearly blind, deaf, and unable to do any work, making it hard for him to keep his wife and five children. He ignored the fact that his oldest child, Bessie, was no longer living at home. However, Aaron's request for an increase was rejected.

The Warrens suffered another setback in May 1911, when the State Land Board disallowed Aaron's placer mining claims on Quartz Creek. His claims were challenged by August Juhre, who contended Aaron was not mining the land, but running cattle. The Land Board agreed, stating that he had not located his claim in good faith. Thus he lost his ranch on Quartz Creek. Without the ranch and in failing health, Aaron left Pierce. He traveled to Orlando, Florida where he was admitted to the sanitarium there in June 1912. He died December 25, 1912, of kidney failure.

After Aaron left for Florida, Mary, too, left Pierce, moving to Peck, Idaho, east of Pierce on the Clearwater River. She opened a boarding house, known as the Monroe House, and also operated a general store. She became well-known in Peck as an honest, capable business woman who turned no one away from her door. She supplemented her income with Aaron's pension for both herself and the children still at home—Harry, Irene, and Charles—although government red-tape delayed payments for almost a year after Aaron's death. In her application for widow's benefits, Mary swore under oath that she had been married only once, to Aaron Warren, and that he was the father of her children.

Mary lived in Peck for the rest of her life. With the exception of Bessie, she remained close to all of her children, even after they left home. William became a banker in Peck, while Harry and Charles (Fred) moved to Lewiston. Emily, her daughter from her first marriage, settled in Orofino, and Irene remained in Peck.

Her only loss was son William who died in 1933 after a short illness.

In the early 1940s, Mary's health began to fail. Bessie Reed learned of her mother's illness from one of her brothers and traveled to Peck to visit her. After twenty years of estrangement, the two settled their differences. Over the next few years, Bessie returned to Peck, taking along several of her children to meet their grandmother. William Reed, however, never accompanied Bessie and never showed any concern about the fate of Mary Warren. She died October 15, 1943, with neither an explanation nor an apology from her son-in-law.

6

A New Life

In the late summer and fall of 1909, while Mary Warren struggled to put her life and marriage back together in Pierce, Reed and Bessie settled into their relationship in Myrtle, Idaho, a small town west of Pierce on the Clearwater River. Destitute because of Reed's legal battles, the couple boarded with a young farmer and his wife, Henry and Ella Kress, and Reed went to work as a stockman. Bessie, three months pregnant, helped around the Kress house and prepared for the birth of her first child.

Samuel O. Reed was born April 20, 1910, a doctor and midwife attending Bessie, who was now fifteen. William Reed, whether out of excitement or confusion, listed the baby's name as William P. on the birth registration. Later a birth certificate would be issued for the child in the name of Samuel Oliver Reed; he would be called Sam.

Sam became Bessie's focal point. Forced to grow up well before her time, she earnestly took on the role of wife and mother. She tended to the needs of her husband and her child. She kept track of her spending on a small tablet, and noted to the penny her expenses. Under the heading of "Baby" she listed the following:

White outing flannel	$1.10
White flannel	$1.30
Long cloth	$2.40
Embroidery	.80

Lawn	$1.20
Lace	.75
Quilts	$1.60
Thread	.25
Lawn	.50
Buttons	.50
Canton Flannel	$1.60
Shirts	$1.00
Olive oil talcum	.50
Soap	.25
Total	$12.75

Bessie also recorded her expenses for the doctor and his assistant. The doctor received $25, while the midwife received five dollars.

After the birth of Sam, Reed continued to work for various ranchers herding stock, and Bessie took care of the baby. Sam was a healthy, happy child, with the piercing eyes of his father and the small stature of his mother. According to Bessie, Reed was pleased that his first child was a son.

The Reeds remained in Myrtle for at least a year after Sam's birth. Then, probably in the late summer of 1911, they packed their few possessions in a wagon and headed to British Columbia. Reed decided to return to Harpers Camp, a place he had enjoyed while working for Union Metallic Cartridge Company.

Harpers Camp, located eighty-one miles west of Prince George on the Horsefly River, was a prime area for trappers. Surrounded by streams and lakes, it was an ideal spot for Reed to make a new start. The location also suited Bessie. She would later recall it was the "prettiest place" they ever lived.

According to information Bessie passed on to her children, the couple settled in a walled tent on a piece of property they planned to homestead. Reed began cutting trees for a cabin, but winter set in before he had an opportunity to finish. Bessie, now

The first picture of Samuel Oliver Reed

pregnant with her second child, was little help. She did, however, continue to keep track of the family's finances which improved in Canada. Reed was a successful trapper, bringing in over $450 during his first season. At the same time, they owned three horses and purchased a cow with a calf and several head of sheep. They also began setting up house, buying a stove and dishes, as well as a table and chair set.

While the tent was drafty and cold, it was home. Here, the Reed's second child, a daughter, was born in December 1911. Bessie was aided by a midwife, Mrs. Ford, who lived nearby. She paid the woman $25 for her services. For his part, Reed named the little girl Mabel, teasing Bessie that the name came from an old girl friend.

The family did well in Harpers Camp until Reed's temper erupted causing an incident that forced them to leave. While neither Bessie nor Reed revealed all the details, Reed apparently used his pistol to beat a Canadian Mountie. Facing arrest, Reed took what possessions he could, and he and his family fled by train from Harpers Camp to The Dalles, Oregon. Upon their arrival in Oregon, Reed purchased a covered wagon and a team of horses. From there, he and his family began a two year odyssey in search of a home.

For a little over a year, the Reeds traveled Oregon, searching for a new home. They spent the winter of 1912 in Prineville, Oregon, then moved on to Fort Rock Desert, Bend, Prairie City, and Burns. Often, they camped in the company of Indians. Bessie found them to be friendly and helpful, especially with the children. They taught her to use large soft leaves as liners in the babies' diapers, making them easier to launder. They also gave her an ointment that could be used to cure diaper rash. Bessie had only one bad experience with the Indian women during her travels. One night, she had hand washed the babies' diapers and hung them over sage brush to dry. When she awoke the next morning, they were gone, snatched by a family of Indians camping near by.

Throughout the spring and early summer of 1913, the Reeds continued their wandering, all the time heading east. Bessie, now expecting her third child, spent her time taking care of the children and preparing for the next one. She bought bolts of flannel and as they traveled, she would sew for the new baby, hemming diapers and blankets, and making dressing gowns. Eventually, they made their way to Idaho, spending time on the shores of Payette Lake, near present day McCall. It was here they learned of available land on Johnson Creek, east of McCall, near Yellow Pine.

The Thunder Mountain Mining Boom of 1901-1902 brought thousands of miners into Idaho's West Central Mountains. When the rush was over, some stayed to homestead in areas around Yellow Pine and on Johnson Creek and the South Fork of the Salmon River. While these settlers continued to work claims, they also ran cattle or freight for the various mining camps still looking for the mother lode. They also did odd jobs for the Forest Service, which got its start in Valley County in 1905 with the creation of the Payette Forest Reserve. They were hardy individuals making a living in a beautiful, but ruggedly remote part of the state.

Reed sensed a golden opportunity. The area was great for trapping so he could immediately support his family. Because it was federal land, he could file a homestead claim and start the ranch he always wanted. He could also do a little prospecting. Better yet, he and his family would be isolated from outsiders and the law; they would be free to go about their lives without outside meddling.

In late August, the family left McCall and traveled a few miles southeast of present-day Cascade to the once bustling town of Thunder City. There they stopped at Logue's General Store and purchased supplies. Then they took the wagon road northeast over Big Creek summit to Knox, a waystation during the Thunder Mountain rush, just north of present day Warm Lake. From there the road continued northeast, over Cabin Creek summit, down Trout Creek to Johnson Creek and on to Yellow Pine. The trip took three days, and when they arrived on Johnson Creek, they found the land they were interested in had already been claimed. Still, Reed and Bessie were intrigued. They liked the country. Game was plentiful, as was timber. Reed could use his trapping prowess to earn an income, then clear an area and start his ranch. They spent the month of September exploring the Johnson Creek area, but could not find a piece that suited them.

With winter approaching and Bessie eight months pregnant, Reed realized he needed to find his family a shelter. They returned to Knox where they rented a cabin near the shores of Warm Lake. Their landlord was Molly Kessler, a colorful pioneer of Long Valley and Knox, who built the first lodge at Warm Lake. Molly would prove invaluable to the Reeds. She not only helped the Reeds prepare for the coming winter, but also served as Bessie's midwife in the birth of Pat Reed, on October 17, 1913. Pat's delivery was long and difficult, and Bessie lost a great deal of blood. Molly is credited with saving Bessie's life by wrapping her in cold sheets to stop the hemorrhaging. She then helped with the children until Bessie was back on her feet.

For his part, Reed went to work trapping. He ran lines up Cabin Creek and Trail Creek and along the South Fork of the Salmon River. Before the snow closed the roads, he ran freight from Cascade to Yellow Pine, and in the winter, he carried the mail from Knox into Yellowpine. While he provided for the family and learned about the country, Bessie took care of the children and settled into their cabin, turning it into a home. She appreciated the roof over her head after two years of living in the wagon.

In the summer of 1914, while working as a fire fighter for the Forest Service, Reed came upon Reeves Bar, an elevated terrace along the east bank of the South Fork of the Salmon River. Located twenty miles north of Knox, the bar was exactly what Reed had in mind: a flat piece of ground with plenty of water, already ditched for irrigation. As an added bonus, an old cabin was on the place. Reed believed it was the ideal place to start his ranch and raise his family.

Reed contacted the Forest Service in McCall to see if the land was available for homesteading. While some of the acreage he sought had been claimed, a portion of it was ready for the taking, and Reed jumped at the chance. Because the site was accessible only by trail, he sold his team and wagon, keeping only his pack horses. Then in August 1914, he and Bessie gathered all the belongings they could carry, tucked the three children—Sam, Mabel, and Pat—into saddle bags, and headed down the South Fork bound for their new home.

7

Claiming the South Fork

The beauty and isolation of the South Fork of the Salmon River are surpassed only by its captivating history, a history that was well-established long before William and Bessie Reed decided to call it home. From tales of Indian battles to those of notorious murders, the stories that flow from the South Fork clearly indicate it was home to hardy pioneers.

The Nez Perce and Mountain Shoshoni Indians, also known as the Sheepeaters, used the South Fork as their summer hunting grounds, attracted to the drainage by the abundant wildlife and magnificent salmon runs. They were joined by the first white men in the 1860s, who came to the area lured by the promise of wealth. After gold was discovered in Warren, Idaho, in 1862, the miners headed southeast, settling along the river, staking claims, and building the first ranches on its bars.

The influx of settlers into Indian lands led to the inevitable. In 1879, a small band of Sheepeaters attacked and killed two miners living at the mouth of Elk Creek. The attacks brought the US Cavalry through South Fork country and eventually into the Middle Fork of the Salmon River drainage where the Sheepeaters were finally subdued. It was a memorable operation, not in its efficiency and success, but from its sheer magnitude.

"We marched 1,258 miles, passed through sections where no

human beings had ever set foot in before," Private Edward Hoffner, Troop G, First Cavalry wrote in his diary concerning the campaign. "[We] Were 117 days in the saddle. A number of animals were made useless, and men badly used up."

With the threat of the Indians eliminated, miners had only to deal with the isolation and profitless claims they found on the South Fork. For all the gold taken out of Warren, Big Creek, and Thunder Mountain, the riches of the South Fork proved much more elusive. Miners staked claims, were disappointed, and moved on. Such was the case of Reeves Bar.

By the time William Reed found Reeves Bar, several hapless individuals had tried their luck there. John Reeves was the first known white settler on Reeves Bar, arriving in the early 1890s. He staked several claims, cleared some of the land, and dug a water ditch from Camp Creek that he used both for irrigation and mining purposes. Reeves eventually abandoned the bar in the early 1900s. He was followed by Paul Forester, a trapper, in 1906. Forester built a small cabin on the south end of the upper bar and used it as his winter headquarters. He left the area in 1907 moving further down river.

In May 1905, William C. Caldwell settled on the lower bar, where both Phoebe Creek and Camp Creek empty into the South Fork. Caldwell was a cantankerous man, whose impatience with the Forest Service and its rules caused problems. A trapper who did some prospecting on the side, Caldwell filed his first application for a homestead in May 1907. He did so under the "June 11 Act," which allowed forest reserves to be opened for homesteading if the land could be put to acceptable agricultural use. In his application, Caldwell stated he had one acre in vegetable cultivation, nine acres in timothy, and fourteen acres of wild hay, enough to support his ten head of horses. He also indicated he had fenced nearly the entire 160 acres he was requesting.

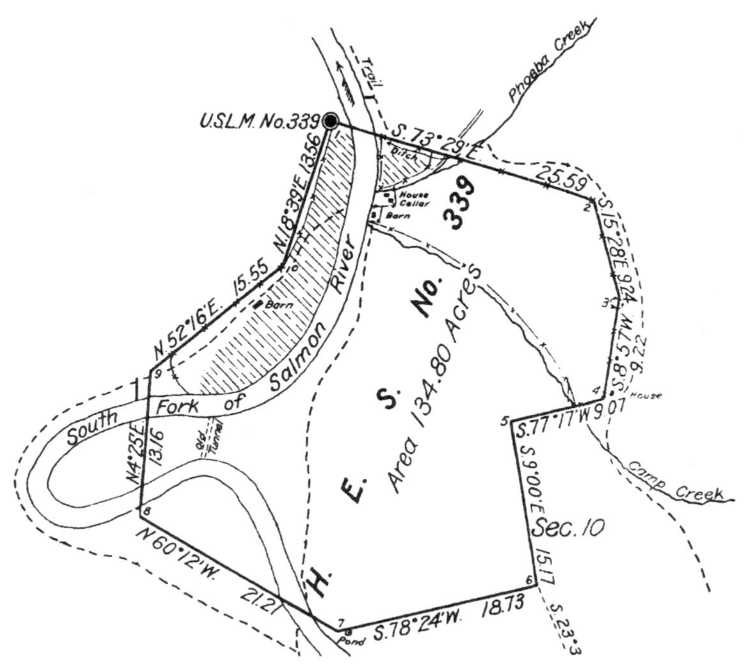

The Caldwell/Tucker Homestead, purchased by Reed in 1920 (USFS)

Forest Service supervisors were suspicious of Caldwell's application, which clearly exaggerated the condition of his homestead. They were slow to respond, causing a flurry of letters from Caldwell. He became even more irritable after his first homestead application was lost. He refiled, but the Forest Service was reluctant to open the heavily timbered land for a homestead. In fact, the Forest Service asserted the land Caldwell requested had been withdrawn for settlement in 1902 because of its timber potential, an estimated one million board feet of Ponderosa Pine.

The feud continued for two years, with Caldwell claiming he had the right to the land, and the Forest Service threatening to charge him for every tree he cut from the property. Forest supervisors in McCall also wanted to refuse his application because it was clear that Caldwell had done no improvements on the property, as mandated by the Homestead Act. Eventually, however, they compromised, and in 1910 Caldwell was given the right to twenty-five acres on lower Reeves Bar adjacent to the river. Caldwell had five years to "prove-up" – make the land usable for agricultural purposes – before he would be given clear title to the land.

Unfortunately for Caldwell, he did not live long enough. In March 1913, in a dispute over a trap line, he was shot and killed by a young trapper named George Wayne. In the aftermath of the shooting, Caldwell's cabin, with him inside, burned to the ground.

Reeves Bar remained empty for a year; then it caught the interest of both Earl Tucker and William Reed. Tucker, however, was the first to file on the piece, staking his claim on the lower bar on January 31, 1914. Either the Forest Service had a change of heart concerning the use of the property, or Tucker was more amenable to them than Caldwell, because his application for 134.8 acres was accepted. Tucker received patent in October 1919.

Reed took up residency on the upper flat, southeast of Tucker's claim in August 1914, moving into a cabin built by miners who had worked claims in the area. Reed added a barn and in the first year cut what hay he could to feed the horses for the winter. He also contacted the Forest Service and let them know of his intent to homestead.

In the summer of 1915, Forest Service officials surveyed Reed's claim and declared the 28.8 acres open for settlement. District Forester A.C. McCain arrived to inspect Reed's plans. He reported that Reed had a good stand of timothy ready to be cut, and that Reed was hoping to bring in twenty-five head of cattle the next summer. However, McCain clearly had his reservations about Reed as he wrote "He is not a practical farmer," and that his garden "did not amount to much."

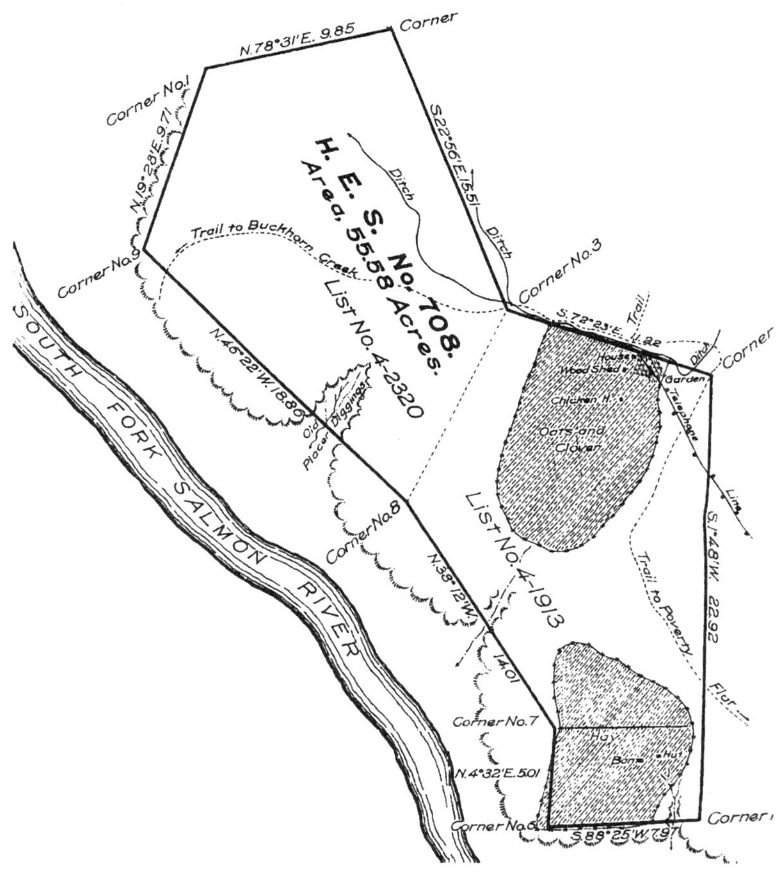

The Forest Service survey showing the land claimed by William Reed

Reed, however, surprised his critics. On April 19, 1916, he officially filed his homestead application which was accepted by the Forest Service. Then, over the next five years, he continued to make progress on his claim. He improved the condition of the main cabin and built an 8′x8′ wood shed, a log chicken coop, and two hay barns. He hand dug a half-mile of irrigation ditch from Camp Creek and irrigated twelve acres of oats, which he used to feed his livestock, a few head of cattle and six horses. He also amended his original homestead application, asking for the adjacent twenty-five acres just northwest of his initial claim, which was granted.

Reed added to his holdings in October 1920 when Tucker sold out. Tucker, who was too ill to work his homestead, offered the property to Reed for $1,200. Somehow, Reed managed to scrape together the funds.

In the summer of 1921, Forest Ranger Walter Estep traveled to the South Fork to inspect Reed's homestead and make his final recommendation. He must have been overwhelmed by the family, however, noting in his report that it consisted of Reed, Bessie, and "five or six small children." Despite his confusion—there were actually seven children at the time—he found that Reed had complied with all of the homestead laws and that the improvements on the property showed he was operating in good faith. Estep filed his final report in January 1922 and in July 1922, Reed received his patent. He and Bessie now owned a little over 188 acres of prime South Fork property, which soon would be known as the Reed Ranch.

Whether by dumb luck or design, Reed had chosen the ideal place to stake his claim. Unlike the rest of the South Fork with its steep terrain, the Reed Ranch was relatively flat, making it ideal for a cattle operation. Water would not be a problem as Phoebe and Camp Creeks were substantial; water would be available year around for domestic use, irrigation, and mining. The creek drainages also attracted wildlife, making the area excellent for trapping. Reed would also not want for timber, as yellow pine was plentiful all around the bar. To top it off, the Reed cabin sat 100 yards from the intersection of three major trails —the Knox Trail, from Warm Lake down the South Fork; the Secesh Trail, north to Warren; and the Cougar/Buckhorn Creek Trail, west to Roseberry. Another trail, less traveled, headed to Yellow Pine. Reed had ready access in and out of his homestead. To him, it was the perfect place.

8

Building the Reed Ranch

When William Reed told Bessie of the South Fork and Reeves Bar, she was elated. She was weary of traveling and tired of depending on the kindness of others. She longed for a place to call her own, where she could raise her family and bring some convention to her life. She knew that life in Idaho's remote back country would be difficult, but her childhood had prepared her for hard work. She wanted to build a home for her family and the South Fork would provide her with that opportunity. She embraced the task ahead.

The twenty mile trip from Warm Lake to Reeves Bar took the Reed family an entire day. The trail was steep and narrow in places, and Bessie followed behind Reed and the pack horses, keeping a close eye on her children tucked tightly in the saddle bags. They carried with them the beginnings of their household—a few pots and pans, the children's clothes, bedding. One saddle horse was piled with Reed's tools and trapping equipment. On another was Bessie's dismantled sewing machine. Staples such as sugar, flour, and beans, enough to get them through the winter, lay across the packs in fifty pound bags.

The cabin on Reeves Bar was little more than a shell when the Reeds arrived. Standing 18′ x 24′, the structure was made of unpeeled yellow pine logs and had a loft, a hard-packed clay floor, and a stone fireplace with a mud chimney. Each sidewall contained a four-paneled window. An old cook stove sat against one wall. When Bessie looked out of the front door of her new home, she looked west to the magnificent view of Tea Pot Dome and Miner's Peak.

They had much work to do to prepare the cabin for winter. The first task was to repair the crumbling chimney. Unsure of how to go about it, they made a concoction of mud and sticks to use as a mortise. When they completed the job, they lit a fire, only to have much of the chimney go up in flames. They managed to extinguish the fire before it caused too much damage and then sought the advice of their neighbor, Tucker. With his help they rebuilt the structure. Later when Bessie told this story to the children, she assured them that their chimney was suitable for Santa Claus, and all the children believed her.

The chimney was just one of the Reeds' worries. The cabin had no furnishings. While they had staples, they had no meat. They had even less money. However, Reed was resourceful; he turned to the one occupation he knew well, trapping.

Reed's homestead was an ideal place for trappers and hunters, a prime winter range for deer. With the deer came other big game, especially cougar and bear. Each fall, this game would travel from the ridges down timbered draws to the South Fork where the meadows provided year round grazing for deer. These game trails were typical sites for trap lines.

Reed set his trap lines in circles, following a game trail up one draw and then returning down another. His traps weighed anywhere from two to five pounds, depending on the animal he was pursuing, and he set one every mile or so. The length of each trap line also varied, running anywhere from five to twenty miles. He would have had a line to the west, running up and down Buckhorn Creek, and another to the east, which followed Phoebe Creek to Indian Ridge and then down Camp Creek. He would check his lines every other day and pack the game back to the cabin.

If Reed were trapping for fur, he would skin the animal, stretch the skin over a board, and set it by the fireplace to dry. Prepared in this way, the hides would keep a long time. In his first year on the South Fork, Reed packed his skins out to Thunder City in the spring and sold them to fur traders. After the establishment of Cascade in 1915, he took his business there. For furs he trapped mink and otter along the South Fork; on the ridges he sought marten and sable, which could bring up to thirty dollars a pelt.

Reed also earned money killing animals for bounty. Government agencies and ranchers would pay hunters and trappers to kill livestock predators such as wolves, cougars, coyotes, and bears. Some were hired by the month to work a certain area, while others were paid by the animal. In the spring of 1915, Reed earned ten dollars for each bear he could kill. Bessie would later recall she used some of this money to buy material to make clothes for the family.

What skins Reed could not sell, he traded to the Indians. Each summer, the Nez Perce would arrive on the South Fork to fish for Chinook salmon. They had a large encampment at the mouth of Cougar Creek, just west of the Reed cabin. They would bring gloves and moccasins to trade in return for hides. By trading with the Indians, Reed always made sure his children had shoes.

He would need many shoes. The Reeds' third son, Bill, was born in August 1915, one year after they arrived at the ranch. Another son, Sandy, followed in February 1917, with Rose, the second daughter, born in October 1918. After Rose came a fifth son, Penny, on July 21, 1920. Three girls followed: Margaret, 1922; Anne, 1924; and Nora, 1926. The eighth child born on the South Fork, a boy, died shortly after birth in May 1929.

With a growing family, Reed turned to other endeavors in addition to his trapping. He learned the area quickly, and because of his knowledge, the Forest Service used him often to fight forest fires and to pack supplies to fire camps and lookouts. Sometimes, when he was packing, he would come upon a rancher who needed a hired hand. He would stop for a few days and bring in cattle, fix fence, or cut hay, whatever was needed. He would return to the South Fork with extra money in his pocket. He also did a little prospecting, and although the South Fork never yielded substantial color, Reed always found enough dust to put a twenty dollar gold piece in his pocket each time he went to Cascade to trade it. He also began working on the ranch, hoping one day to make it pay. He dug irrigation ditches across the bar and planted twelve acres of oats. In 1916, he was granted a grazing permit for fifty head of cattle. To start his herd, he brought in a cow with a calf, which also provided fresh milk for the family. This was short lived, however. In the fall a large fire was burning in the area, and the Forest Service sent crews to fight it. The crews needed food, and so the camp cook turned to Reed. Reed sold him the cow, but Bessie was none too happy when she found out what Reed had done. To her, milk for the children was more important than money.

The following year Reed trailed in a few more head of cattle and some sheep. He also brought in a saw mill, which would come in handy as he expanded his homestead. He built two hay sheds, a chicken coop, and a wood shed. He also continued to trap and hunt and earned the reputation as one of the finest marksmen on the South Fork. This reputation was reinforced when packages of ammunition from Remington Steel addressed to "Deadshot" Reed began arriving for him in Cascade. Although he had done nothing up to this time on the South Fork to gain notoriety, he encouraged the persona of the Texas cowboy with his Ranger stories, his cowboy politeness, and his sometimes ruthless disposition. It was not long until everyone in Valley County either knew or had a story about Deadshot.

The life of Reed was much different from that of Bessie. While he moved around a great deal on the South Fork, tending his trap lines and cattle, leaving the area for Yellow Pine, Big Creek, Knox, or Cascade, Bessie remained at the cabin. At first, she helped him around the homestead, tending to the animals, bringing in Chinook salmon to smoke or pickle, as the Indians taught her. She also took care of the family finances, keeping track of Reed's take from his fur trade. It was Bessie who filled out the reports for Remington Steel, working with Reed as he tried out a box of new bullets or a new gun.

But with each new baby, Bessie spent less time working on the ranch and more time looking after children and the house. Every day she lived at the South Fork, from 1915 to 1929, at least one of her children was in diapers. Much of the time she cared for them by herself as Reed was often away trapping or packing for the Forest Service. Bessie, however, was up to the task. Relying on the skills she learned at her parents' hotel, she managed the family, delegating chores, giving the more difficult ones to Sam, Mabel, and Pat. Even the youngest were given tasks, and Bessie expected them done. In this way, the family not only survived, it flourished.

If Bessie ever despaired over her situation, she kept those feelings to herself. Instead she poured herself into raising her children, making sure they were clean, fed, and loved. She also stood by her husband, whose behavior at times tested her will. Later in her life she would recall the years on the South Fork as her best. All of the children would concur.

9

Family Life

Life on the South Fork for the Reeds was much like the lives of other families trying to survive in Idaho's back country. The hard work and the isolation made for tough times. What made the Reeds different, however, was their sheer numbers and the dominating personality of William Reed. All of these elements would shape the lives of the children born and raised on the Reed Ranch.

At first, Bessie had time to spend with her children, and she made the most of it, giving them the attention they needed. According to her daughter Anne, she gave hugs freely and always made her children feel wanted. She was also a task master. Even though they were small—Sam was just four and Mabel three—she gave them small jobs to do. Sam was in charge of his sister and brother, keeping track of them as his mother cleaned or cooked. Mabel helped by gathering apples that had fallen from the trees near the house. Both attempted to pack water to the cabin from the ditch that ran nearby. Mostly the water ended up on the ground or on them, but Bessie was patient. At night, Bessie would tuck all three children into a straw bed that lay on the floor of the cabin. Sometimes she would read to them or recite poetry. Reed was often gone on his trap lines or packing trips, so it would just be Bessie and the children. She cherished these quiet times.

Reed also enjoyed the children when they were small. He especially loved them when they were babies, spending time to

An early picture of Bessie and her children in front of their South Fork cabin. Shown here are, left to right, Sandy, Rose, Bessie (holding Penn) Mabel, and Sam.

coddle and rock them at night. He delivered every child born at the Reed Ranch, eight in all, losing only one. At first, he and Bessie were on their own, but by 1920, when Penny was born, Mabel was able to assist, heating water and blankets for both her mother and the newborn. Before the birth of each child, Reed always told Bessie that he wanted to have a boy, and he was pleased when he delivered Bill, Sandy, and Penny. But he was no less attentive when he delivered Rose, Margaret, Anne, and Nora. In fact, had he not been so vigilant, he would have lost Nora. Margaret later recalled that "Dad had to work on Nora a long time" in order to get the little girl to breathe.

As for the names of the children, Bessie named all of the boys, while Reed chose the names for the girls. None of the girls were given middle names. Later in their lives, when they received delayed birth certificates from Valley County, they were allowed to choose their own. Rose chose "Mae," after Mae West, a name she read on a magazine lining the walls of the cabin. Anne selected the name "Narcissus," after being goaded by her father, a big name for a little girl.

With her growing brood, Bessie put to use the organizational skills she had learned while working in her parents' hotel. The children had a strict regimen of morning chores that had to be completed before they were released to go explore the perimeters of the Reed ranch. The children remembered Bessie as the perfect drill sergeant as she ran the household with military precision. Each morning, Sam's job was to start the fires in the cook stove and fireplace while Pat went out to check on the animals. Mabel helped wash and dress her younger brothers and sisters and then set the table for breakfast. As more little Reeds were added to the work force, Bessie increased their duties. Sandy and Bill hauled water, and Rose and Penn milked the cows. Each morning fresh bread came out of the oven, compliments of Bessie and the girls.

Laundry was also a family affair. With a child in diapers every year the Reeds lived on the South Fork, Bessie needed the older children's help to keep up with the washing. First, however, the family had to make soap, a concoction of lye and bear grease. Bessie saved the ashes from her cook stove in a hopper, and by pouring water over the ashes, she would create liquid lye. Then, over an outdoor fire stoked continually by the boys, she would render the bear grease, mixing it with water and boiling it all day to get rid of impurities. She would then let the mixture cool until she had pure bear grease floating on top which she skimmed. Then after disposing of the liquid, she would return the bear grease to the pot and add the lye. She would bring this mixture to a boil. As the concoction began to thicken, she would add common salt. The job was complete when the mixture formed a frothy ball which she would pour into a small washtub. After the soap cooled, she removed it from the tub and cut it into squares to be used for all cleaning purposes. Thus, with soap in hand, the family tackled the laundry.

The boys were in charge of packing the water, which they heated in big pots on the stove. Using an old washboard and two wash tubs, Bessie would soap up the clothes in one tub and then drop them into the rinse water in the other. Rose and Mabel would hang the clothes on a line strung from the cabin to a nearby tree. In this way, the babies had clean diapers and the family had clean clothes. This was important to Bessie who, even in the worst circumstances, was particular about her appearance. She was always neat and tidy and wanted her children and her home to be the same. Reed was also fastidious about his appearance, especially his clothes. When he returned from tending his trap lines or leading a pack trip, he demanded that Bessie have a clean shirt waiting for him. He never traveled to Cascade, Knox, or Yellow Pine without a newly laundered shirt on his back.

All of the clothes worn by the Reeds, including Deadshot's shirts and the boys' jeans, were made by Bessie. Using her Singer sewing machine, she could turn out a night shirt or a dress in no time. Most of the clothes were made of denim, which Reed would buy by the bolt on his trips to Cascade. The babies' clothes, nightshirts, and some of the girls' dresses were made of flannel, also bought by the bolt. On occasion, Reed would come back with printed material. This would delight Bessie who would make herself or one of the older girls a new dress. Not all the clothes, however, came from store-bought material. Bessie let nothing go to waste, and when a fifty pound flour or oatmeal sack was empty, she promptly turned it into someone's new shirt or dress. Bessie passed her skills on to Mabel and Rose, and in time they

From left to right: Rose, Pat, Sandy, Bill, Mabel, and Sam. All of the children are barefoot.

helped with the mending and sewing.

If Bessie could not make what they needed, she turned to the Montgomery Ward catalog. She and the children poured over all the items in the catalog, dreaming of store-bought fancy clothes, toys, and fine kitchen items. While they knew they could never order such treasures, they enjoyed the make-believe. Bessie did order the children's shoes and the girls' Christmas presents. She would buy doll faces and then sew the rest of the dolls herself using scraps of material. Each year the girls would find new dolls under the Christmas tree. The catalog also served another useful purpose. When a new catalog arrived, the old one would be put to use. Bessie made a paste of water and flour, and she and the children would spend time papering the walls of the cabin. They also used other paper and magazines, whatever they could find. In this way, they not only cleaned the cabin walls, but also insulated them as well. When they left the South Fork in 1929, twelve layers of paper lined the walls.

Bessie also taught the older girls to cook, and there was no shortage of food in the Reed household. Game was plentiful in the late winter and spring on the South Fork, and Bessie prepared it in a variety of ways, including canning and drying it to use during any lean times. From the river, the family took salmon and whitefish, which they either smoked or pickled. Four apple trees grew less than 100 feet from the cabin, and each fall Bessie would can or dry the fruit the children had gathered. The children also picked huckleberries, which Bessie preserved. What could not be obtained from the land, Reed purchased on his trips to Cascade. At least twice a year he packed in flour, sugar, salt, coffee, oatmeal, and cornmeal, all in fifty pound bags. The oatmeal was a special treat for Bessie who craved it during her pregnancies. She always had a handful of oatmeal in her apron pocket.

While Bessie was in charge of the household, Reed controlled the homestead. He, too, put the children to work. However, unlike Bessie, who was patient and kind, Reed was demanding and cruel. The father who had been so gentle with his children as babies turned into a mean-spirited brute as soon as they were old enough to walk and talk. The children learned quickly to do what they were told, and do it well, or there would be hell to pay.

One of the first things Reed taught all his children was how to handle a gun. He spent hours with them, teaching them how to care for and clean a gun as well as how to shoot. Every one of the children became a crack shot and, while on the South Fork, Reed put their skills to the test. At random, he would call on one of the boys to go out and shoot something for dinner. Then he would give his son just one bullet. If the son came back empty-handed, depending on Reed's mood, he could get anywhere from a lecture to a beating. The lesson was incentive for all the children to learn to be good shots. The strategy, while cruel, did pay off, as Reed was often gone for long periods and the children would have to hunt for their supper.

When Reed was home, he did not have much to do with his children, except when it came to work. As the boys got older, he expected them to tend the trap lines with him, which they did. They all learned the ways of the woods, to track and trap animals, to hunt, and to fish. But they also had to work the ranch, building and mending fence, tending to the animals, digging irrigation ditches, and cutting hay. But no matter how hard they tried to please their father, it was often not good enough.

Sam and Pat had it especially rough on the South Fork. As the oldest boys, Reed expected them to do much of the work. He forced them to work side by side with him, doing the labor of grown men. He could not understand that they were still children, and when they were unable to meet his demands, he became violent. Using his hat, the back of his pistol, or a bull whip, he would hit them, leaving welts and bruises all over their bodies. Sometimes the damage was worse. When Sam was ten years old, he was helping his father shore up a flume that took water from Camp Creek across the bar by the cabin. The flume collapsed; Reed hit Sam so hard, that Sam was knocked cold. According to Mabel, he was unconscious until the next day.

Reed's temper was volcanic. He would erupt quickly, blasting the boy who had caused his wrath. Then just as suddenly, his anger would subside, and he would return to normal, oblivious to the damage he had caused. Bessie was livid when the boys would come to the cabin, welts covering their backs and legs. She would treat their wounds, and then square off against Reed. He would respond with a tirade, but in all their years of marriage, he never struck her. She could calm him in a way no one else could. While she could never get him to stop beating the boys, whenever she was present he never laid a hand on them. The problem was that she could not protect them all the time.

The girls escaped the physical damage inflicted on the boys. While Reed gave his daughters a quick swat or spanking whenever they disobeyed his rules, he never hit them about the head or with his whip. Instead, they weathered his verbal attacks, as did their mother. Still they were afraid of him and did their best to avoid him. The sisters also had an unwritten pact they shared: no one would ever be alone with him.

Still, they could not avoid their father. When Reed was home, he held center court, especially at meal time. The family had supper on a long pine table with benches at either side. Reed sat

The children stand in front of their cabin. Left to right are Sandy, Bill, Rose, Penny, Pat, and Sam.

at one end, and Bessie sat at the other, a tradition that continued long after the Reeds moved from the South Fork. The conversation was controlled by Reed, and the children could only speak when spoken to. If the children requested another helping, they were sure to use their best manners. It was at these family suppers that Reed would tell the children stories of his early life. Daughters Ruth and Anne both believe their father greatly embellished the stories, especially those of his gun fights and life as a Texas Ranger. But the stories made an impression; nobody crossed their father.

Reed's presence at the ranch meant the children did as they were told. Orders were given, and they did their best to execute them. But most of the time, they stayed out of their father's way. As the family grew, all the children except the youngest and Sam, who built the morning fire, slept in a walled tent near the cabin. Each morning they would make their way into the cabin, sit down for breakfast, and find out their chores for the day. Once their chores were completed, they were free to be children.

From the river to the trails, to the abandoned cabins to the wildlife, the children turned the South Fork into their playground. Baby chipmunks became household pets, fed and tamed by the children who packed them around in their pockets. Abandoned cabins, although forbidden by their father, were meant to be explored for the unknown treasures they might hold. Neighbors were also fair game, and the Reeds struck up a lasting relationship with Bill Darling, a prospector, who lived two miles upriver on Bells Bar. Darling befriended the entire Reed family, but was especially kind to the children, who saw him as a surrogate father. Several of the Reed children kept in touch with Darling long after they moved from the South Fork.

If the children got into trouble, they were left to their own designs to get out of it, as Bessie was too busy minding the ba-

All that is left of the milkhouse built by Sam and Pat

bies to keep track of everybody. She took comfort knowing that the children stuck together and, for the most part, got along. Although they were competitive, the rivalries were healthy and they seldom fought. They played cards, jumped rope, and played hopscotch; they also at times let their curiosity get the best of them.

One such instance involved Rose, Penny, and Margaret, who decided to explore the old Tucker cabin on the north end of the ranch. While the Tucker place was off limits, the children could not resist. Penn put a halter on "Big Foot," an old pack horse the kids liked to ride, and the three youngsters took off. Once they reached Camp Creek, they left the horse and continued on foot until they reached the abandoned cabin. In their exploration, Margaret fell through the floor, cutting her leg on an old nail. Crying, she begged Penn to bring the horse to carry her home, but the horse had already made his way back to the ranch. Margaret remembered the walk home being "awful," not only because of her pain, but because of the punishment they knew was waiting for them.

Curiosity also got the best of Rose when she tried her first cigarette, compliments of her brothers Penn and Sandy. The two boys had been out exploring and stumbled across a sheepherder's camp. They could not resist stealing some Bull Durham and a wild west magazine, which they offered to share with their sisters. The boys rolled the cigarettes and then passed them around. Rose became violently ill. As they headed home, she told the others she was going to the milk house to lie down and "die." When the children showed up without Rose, Bessie badgered them to find out what had happened. She found Rose still in the milk house; Bessie spent a long time convincing Rose that she was not going to die.

While the younger children were free to explore the South Fork, Pat and Sam spent much of their time working the ranch, taking care of the cattle, fixing fence, repairing ditches. They also took on additional tasks, many of them to please their mother. One job they tackled was building a wood floor for the cabin. They cut several straight poles and laid them down on the original hard clay floor. Then they found several straight grained fir trees which they cut into three-foot blocks. Using a rip saw, they cut shakes from the blocks, which they nailed to the wooden poles. In this way, Bessie got a real floor in the cabin. The boys also built the milk house, a log structure which spanned the irrigation ditch that ran by the cabin. The icy waters of Camp Creek kept the structure cool. Here the family would store their milk, hang their homemade sausage, and store the barrels that held their pickled whitefish.

Besides taking care of the ranch, Sam and Pat kept busy in the winter trapping. They became excellent trackers and were always on the lookout for new areas in which to set their trap lines. On one such scouting trip, the boys stumbled on to a set of tracks they did not recognize. When they described them to their father, Reed told them they were the prints of a Canadian lynx. Since lynx were unheard of in South Fork country, Pat and Sam decided they must have the animal. Gathering a few essentials, their snow shoes, and a couple of dogs, the boys set off. They tracked the lynx for three days, through heavy snows, before taking shelter for one night in an abandoned cabin on Caton Creek. Then the next day they were off again, following the trail. After three more nights of eating roasted snow shoe rabbits and sleeping in snow caves, they decided to call it quits. They made their way to a cabin on Johnson Creek where an old prospector took them in, warmed them up, and fed them corn meal. The prospector contacted Clark Cox, at the Cox Ranch, who in turn contacted the Reeds, to let them know the boys were okay. The next day, with their bellies full and much humbled, they headed home.

While the children received lessons in survival each day on the Reed Ranch, their formal education was another story. Not only did the isolation of the ranch prohibit them from going to school, but Reed himself saw no value in education. He felt people were better off working from dawn until dusk. Bessie, however, believed the children needed an education. At first, she taught the children herself. She spent time with Sam, Mabel, and Pat, teaching them their letters and numbers. But as more children came along, she had less time to spend with each one. Bessie worried they would suffer when they were adults because they had no formal schooling.

The Reed children's first introduction to public education came in 1920, when the entire family moved to Knox to spend the winter. From October to May, the family rented a cabin while Sam, Mabel, and Pat attended school. Living in Knox was not Reed's idea, but Idaho's compulsory education laws and Valley

County officials encouraged Reed to put his children in school. He obliged for one year, but in April, even before the school term was over, Reed moved his family back to the South Fork.

In the late fall of 1922, the Reeds moved to Yellow Pine. Sam, Mabel, Pat, and Bill enrolled in school, where they made up one quarter of the enrollment. However, in early spring, Reed once again gathered his family and returned to the ranch. Determined to see her children get an education, Bessie borrowed books and lessons from the Yellow Pine teacher, Mark Lawton, and began the arduous task of homeschooling her children. Each night after supper, when all the day's work was completed, she would sit at the pine table with her children and instruct them in reading, writing, and arithmetic. She would send their papers to the teacher in Yellow Pine to be marked.

They returned to Yellow Pine in the fall of 1927 and moved into the deserted cabin of Henry Abstein, an early Yellow Pine homesteader. Each morning the children—Sam, Mabel, Pat, Penny, Rose, Sandy, and Bill, Jr.—made the one mile walk to school. Sam and Mabel were in charge of getting the group to school on time, not always an easy task. Sam would lead and Mabel would bring up the rear. As soon as Mabel was out of sight of the Abstein cabin and the watchful eye of her mother, she would cut a willow stick. Then, if one of the children got out of line or dawdled at all, she would use the switch to keep the kids moving. According to Lafe Cox, who went to school with the Reed clan, Mabel kept them "tight to the rigging" all the way to school.

Reed would spend only two or three days a week in Yellow Pine. Instead he would be back on the South Fork tending his stock or checking his trap lines. The boys also continued to trap. Sam and Pat had a line that ran down Johnson Creek while Penny and Sandy worked the East Fork, west of Yellow Pine.

The Reeds remained in Yellow Pine for the entire school term, and that spring Sam graduated from the eighth grade. It would be the last of his public education. That summer, Sam went to work for the Forest Service and was stationed on Blackmare Lookout, just west of Poverty Flats. The rest of the family returned to the ranch.

Such was the life of the Reeds, who made a name for themselves on the South Fork. Of course, their number made some take notice, but others were more taken with Bessie's ability to raise the children, who were well mannered and extremely polite. Others were impressed by Reed's hunting and trapping skills, which he passed along to the boys. Mostly, however, people were taken by Deadshot's demeanor, his irascible behavior when things did not go his way, and the tales of his past. Later, after his confrontation with George Krassel, the stories reached legendary proportion.

10

Killing Krassel

In the spring of 1914, George Krassel, a German immigrant, wandered into Central Idaho and the South Fork country. A placer miner, Krassel first eyed the Tucker place at the mouth of Phoebe and Camp Creeks, but finding Tucker firmly entrenched there, he traveled further downriver to Indian Creek. There he built the first cabin on what was known as Dutchman's Bar, located across Indian Creek from the present day Krassel Ranger Station.

Krassel staked a claim, the Rhubarb Placer, and also worked for the Forest Service on occasion, building trail and serving as a Forest Guard. He would often pass by the Reed Ranch on his way to Knox or McCall, and in this way, he became acquainted with Reed and the family. The relationship was not at all cordial.

Both Reed and Krassel were bull-headed and ornery. They took an instant dislike to each other from their first meeting, which took place as early as 1914. Both were territorial, and both wanted the Tucker homestead. Adding fuel to the fire was their propensity to argue over everything, from cattle grazing to mining claims to World War I.

Krassel was a proud German, and with the outbreak of hostilities in Europe in 1914, he was often heard to boast of the superiority of the German people and their first-class war machine. He was convinced that by the end of the war, Germany would have complete control of Europe. On his trips into McCall or

Cascade, Krassel would get the latest international news and then return to the back country to put his spin on the current events. His constant bravado irritated Reed.

Prior to the United States' entry into World War I, Reed and Krassel had merely argued over the politics of the time, but after the US declared war on Germany, the relationship between the two men became much more heated. Krassel took great delight in sharing his war views, especially when Germany held the upper hand. On one such occasion, he took his smugness a bit too far. In December 1917, Krassel was returning to Indian Creek after picking up his mail in Knox. He stopped by the Reed Ranch where he informed Reed that the latest news indicated the Germans were going to win the war. This led to an angry exchange, with each man swearing to kill the other. Krassel reached for his rifle, but Reed drew his six-gun before Krassel could square up for a shot. The confrontation ended at a stalemate, but the animosity between the two would continue to fester.

News of the Krassel-Reed altercation hit the newspapers in January 1918, when the *Cascade News* reported the possible killing of George Kessler [sic] by Dead Shot [sic] Reed. According to the paper, rumors and reports indicated Reed shot Krassel on "about Dec. 22" and then buried the body. The newspaper later retracted the story, indicating that Krassel was alive and well.

So was the feud. Krassel related the incident to his friends, insisting Reed had pulled his gun and threatened to kill him without any provocation. Reed countered that Krassel had started the argument. Krassel also told his friends and several Forest Service Rangers that he was going to "exterminate that Reed family, kill the whole works of them." The threats bothered Bessie, who was often alone at the ranch with the children. She kept a wary eye out for the German.

Tensions heightened when Germany lost the war, a fact Reed enjoyed sharing with Krassel. Krassel only made matters worse when he moved onto the Tucker claim in the spring of 1919. Tucker, who expected to receive a patent on his homestead later that year, was ill with Bright's Disease, a kidney ailment. He often left his claim to seek medical attention, asking friends to look after his stock and homestead. Krassel was more than happy to oblige. He wanted to be first in line if Tucker's health forced him to sell out.

Krassel now lived within shouting distance of the Reeds, but the two men were not neighborly. Reed made no attempt to keep his cattle out of Tucker's fields. The stock trailed down to the river, both north and south of the Reed cabin, crossing onto Tucker's property, where they fed on his hay fields and broke down his fences, all left in the care of Krassel. Krassel quickly tired of the trespass and decided to confront Reed.

In the early morning of June 26, 1919, Krassel mounted his old white horse and, armed with his Savage rifle, rode bareback three quarters of a mile to the Reed cabin. Wearing a black duster, he hid the rifle next to his left leg, underneath the long coat. He made his way east, riding from Tucker's lower meadow up toward the Reed's. Bessie, busy with morning chores, just happened to look out the door and saw a man riding toward the cabin. She immediately recognized Krassel.

Bessie watched him closely. As he approached the irrigation ditch that ran across the meadow, he turned his horse north and followed it for several yards. Then he jumped the horse across the ditch. In doing so, he revealed his rifle, and Bessie knew she needed to warn her husband.

Reed was northeast of the cabin on Camp Creek, listening for his horses, something he did each morning. Sam and Pat were just coming in from having checked on the band of sheep the family kept bedded near the house. The two boys had moved them southeast of the cabin onto the hill behind the meadow. They had just returned for breakfast when Bessie noticed Krassel.

Bessie did not hesitate. She found Reed's Colt. 45, wrapped it in her apron, and gave it to Mabel. Mabel was to find her father, give him the gun, and warn him that Krassel had come calling with his rifle. Bessie gave strict instructions for the rest of the children to stay out of sight in the cabin, but Pat sneaked out onto the front porch and hid in a corner where he had a good view "watching the show," as he later put it.

Krassel was sitting on his horse in front of the cabin when Reed appeared. Reed spoke first, and then an argument ensued concerning Reed's cattle. Krassel threatened to poison Reed's stock that constantly destroyed his crops. As Krassel protested, he took his rifle out from under his duster and laid it across his lap. Reed would later tell the authorities that all the time the two were talking, Krassel was working to take the safety off the rifle. At one point, Krassel looked down at the gun, and Reed guessed he was about to fire, so he took several steps sideways. Krassel swung his rifle toward Reed and fired once. He missed. As he jacked another shell into the chamber, Reed fired his pistol. The bullet struck Krassel in the chest, and he fell from his horse. As he hit the ground, so did his rifle, which fired once more, a harmless shot into the air.

Krassel was dead, a bullet through his heart. Reed took the German's horse and tied it to a fence post nearby. Then he went into the cabin and using the phone the Forest Service had installed to facilitate back country communication, he called Sheriff Ed Smith in Cascade to tell him the story. Following the phone call, he and Bessie found an old piece of canvas, covered the body of Krassel, and waited for the sheriff to arrive.

Smith, accompanied by the county's prosecuting attorney and coroner, immediately drove to Knox. From there, the three men borrowed horses and rode down the South Fork trail to the Reed

Ranch, arriving there around 9 p.m. The body of Krassel still lay where it fell.

The next morning, the coroner examined Krassel's body and the prosecuting attorney questioned Reed about the incident. The coroner then convened an inquest and found that "Krassel came to his death by a pistol-shot wound, the gun being in the hand of W.L. Reed, we believe in self-defense."

Following the inquest, the three officials buried the body northwest of the Reed cabin, on the property line between the Reed and Tucker homesteads. They then returned to Cascade where they made their reports.

The shooting made the front page in the Cascade and McCall newspapers, with both giving much ink to the feud between the two men. The McCall paper, the *Payette Lake Star,* in particular, noted Krassel had predicted Reed would kill him. The *Star* concluded its article by proclaiming that Deadshot was unconcerned about the matter and that the shooting of Krassel was "said to be his fourth killing."

It was one more tale to add to the growing legend of Deadshot Reed.

11

The Legend Grows

Even before the shooting of Krassel, the reputation of Deadshot Reed was well-established in the repertoire of Idaho's story tellers. Spurred by exaggeration and innuendo, the tales overshadowed his actual abilities as an excellent trapper and marksman. The stories he shared with others concerning his life prior to Idaho only added to his notoriety.

It was common knowledge that Reed was an ex-Texas Ranger, forced to kill desperate men in desperate times. Reed relished the embellishment and did little to dissuade storytellers from making him seem larger than life. In one particular story of his Texas days, he was forced to defend the honor of a young woman. He had accompanied her to a dance hall, and when another man made unwanted advances against her, Reed called him out. The result was a shootout that left the man dead. In another, Reed was taking a prisoner for trial in San Antonio. A group of vigilantes surrounded him; they wanted to hang the prisoner on the spot. Reed refused to give in, and when the dust cleared, only Reed and the prisoner were left standing.

Other stories concerned his cattle rustling altercation in Pierce. While newspapers from Pierce and Lewiston gave reasonably accurate accounts of the entire affair, the tales that circulated for years after the incident were much more colorful. In one, Reed had been arrested in Orofino and was awaiting his transfer to Lewiston. Handcuffed, Reed accompanied the sheriff into a restaurant where they were to have lunch and wait for the

Idaho Governor Baldridge shoots a picture of his hunting party. Reed is kneeling in front. (Photo by Ansgar Johnson)

train. Reed managed to overpower the guard, steal his gun, and make a clean getaway. In another version, Reed actually killed a man in the shootout. When the *Lewiston Morning Tribune* classed Reed as "a bad man," the rumors that followed simply supported the claim.

These altercations, along with others, reportedly were the cause of Reed's escape to the South Fork. According to the stories, the South Fork was his hideout, a place where few could find him and he could protect his family. Reed spoke of desperadoes from his Texas Ranger days who looked to get their revenge. He also disparaged the Carrs, sure they would come after him. With each year, he became more paranoid that someone from his past would hunt him down and kill him or one of his children. He developed the habit of never turning his back to anyone. If Reed met another person on the trail, he would step aside and watch the person until he was out of sight.

Reed's paranoia kept him from the demon that often plagued people in the back country. He never drank. Because he believed he was a hunted man, he knew it was important to keep his wits about him. He did not frequent bars, even though stories to that effect circulated around Cascade and McCall. He also kept no alcohol in his home, save for one bottle of whiskey. This he used to cure sore throats, tooth aches, and other assorted physical ailments. According to his daughter Ruth, the children often feigned sore throats in order to have a little taste of "the medicine."

But if Reed was actually concerned about keeping a low profile and hiding his identity, his conduct did little to support it. He only added to his notoriety with his contentious behavior that became well known throughout the area.

Reed spent much of his time in the summers packing for the Forest Service. He knew the South Fork country well, and he had a capable pack string that allowed him to carry ample supplies to the lookouts and ranger stations. One summer, he was called to pack into a large fire burning east of the South Fork. He was accompanied by a Forest Service employee, Bob Wallace of Donnelly, who at the time was just a teenager. They put together a string of 15 horses, all heavily loaded, and headed into the back country, with Reed in the front and Wallace in the back. The weather was hot, the trail was narrow, and the terrain was steep. One of the horses in the middle of the string acted up, bucking and kicking, which agitated the other horses. Reed stopped the string and moved the horse to a different position, but it did no good. Fed up, Reed went to the horse, removed its gear, and shot it in the head. He then rolled it down the mountain. Wallace, who witnessed the entire scene, was terrified. The rest of the trip he stayed at the back of the pack and did not say a word. He later told the story to other Forest Service employees, and the story spread.

Eventually, Reed became a legend in Valley County. People who faced him on the street crossed to the other side to avoid any type of confrontation, no matter how small. Fish and Game officials always approached his cabin warily, for fear of setting him off, as Reed often greeted them with gun in hand. But even in their fear, people respected the hunting and tracking skills of William Reed. When Idaho Governor H. Clarence Baldridge decided go hunting in Idaho's wilderness, Reed was one of those called to lead the way.

In October 1927, Baldridge, along with Harry Shellworth, an executive of the Boise Payette Lumber Company, and Richard Rutledge, Regional Forester from Salt Lake, among others, traveled to Central Idaho. The governor's purpose, according to the *Idaho Statesman,* was to get firsthand information about increased game numbers in the areas surrounding Warren and Edwardsburg (Big Creek). Baldridge and his entourage explored the area for four weeks, hunting and fishing the tributaries of both the South and Middle Forks of the Salmon River. They were guided by the best hunters in the area, including Deadshot Reed.

Governor Baldridge poses with his hunting party. Baldridge stands in the middle of the group. Reed is in the back row, third from the left. (Photo by Ansgar Johnson)

Ansgar Johnson, a well-known Boise photographer, was along to document the governor's trip. His pictures show the governor and his party, along with some of their kills, and the men who helped them in their successful hunt. If Reed's intention was to hide out on the South Fork, his cover was certainly blown when a full page of Johnson's pictures, including two of Reed, appeared in the Nov. 7, 1927 edition of the *Idaho Statesman.* In the pictures, he is the only man not smiling or waving to the camera.

12

Selling the South Fork

Despite Reed's notoriety and unpredictable behavior, he and his family thrived on the South Fork. They had a roof over their heads, plenty of food to eat, and clothes to keep them warm. While they by no means had a life of luxury, they were able to pay their bills with Reed's earnings from trapping and various Forest Service jobs.

In Reed's early years on the river, his mining activity was fairly limited. Prior to 1926, the children worked the streams with their pans and sluice boxes; Reed simply gave directions and took whatever gold they happened to find, which was not much. But in April 1926, Reed was in Cascade to stake his first official claim, the Oxbow, located on the South Fork, due west from his cabin. Three months later, he staked four more—the Big Rock, Cougar Creek, Martin Creek, and South Fork claims. The following summer, he signed Bessie's name on two claims, Phoebe Creek and Reeves Bar, and he filed three more in his name, Camp Creek, Timothy Patch and Jakie Gulch.

It is difficult to know if Reed's sudden interest in mining was just coincidence or part of a well-designed plan. He surely knew that others before him had mined along the South Fork without much success and that areas near Yellow Pine, Big Creek, and Thunder Mountain were more lucrative than the South Fork. He also knew that "a sucker is born every minute," and perhaps he thought he could reel in a few.

From the early 1920s, Reed had been continually pressured

This photo was probably taken in 1928. Marge and Penn are in the front row while Sandy, Bill, and Rose are in the middle. In the back stands Mabel (holding Anne), Pat, and Sam.

to enroll his children in public schools. Supported by Idaho's compulsory education laws, the Valley County Sheriff contacted Reed each year, urging him to follow the law. Most of the time Reed ignored the intrusions into his family's life, but in 1927, he reconsidered and sent his children to the Yellow Pine school, only to withdraw them the next year. The removal prompted several visits from county officials who demanded that Reed send the children to school. Realizing he was in a situation he could not control, Reed decided it was time to sell the homestead.

There was little demand for land on the South Fork, especially when it was accessible only by pack trail. But mining claims were different. If Reed could convince someone that the ranch and his mining claims held good promise, he could demand a price that could buy him a real cattle operation, the kind he always desired, somewhere near a town with a school. Then the county officials would leave him alone.

In the summer of 1928, Reed made several trips into Cascade, each time taking gold he allegedly found on his claims. He flaunted his good fortune up and down the river, trying to get the attention of investors who believed gold could be in the area. Eventually, several Nampa businessmen who frequently hunted in the South Fork took an interest. They sent in surveyors to check out the property and Reed's claims.

Reed was not going to disappoint them. According to Herb Baker, one of the surveyors, Reed took them down to the river where he showed them one of his claims. In a demonstration, he took a pan of gravel from the river, and when he was done, it showed clear signs of color. Baker was suspicious, and later he tried to replicate Reed's feat but was unsuccessful. He believed, as did others in the area, that Reed was "salting" his claims. Baker, however, did not report his findings to the Nampa investors. Instead, probably fearful of Deadshot's reaction, yet not wanting to be involved in the ruse, he quit his surveying job.

Baker was working in Cascade on Oct. 29, 1928, the day the Reeds sold all of their property to the South-Salmon Placer Mining Company of Nampa. While the official record lists the sale price as "one dollar and other good and valuable considerations," Baker, who witnessed the sale, reported Reed received $10,000 in cash for his property. The children would later remember the amount as $15,000. Whatever the total, Reed's investment on the South Fork proved profitable; he had enough money in his pocket to move his family and start the cattle operation he had always wanted.

As part of the agreement, the family remained on the South Fork for another year. Reed continued to pack and run his trap lines, but he also made plans for the move. In late April, he and Mabel traveled to the Emmett area where he checked out ranches and pasture land. Bessie, who was eight months pregnant, stayed behind to care for the children. Shortly after Reed's return, Bessie went into labor. On May 25, she gave birth to a boy, her eleventh child. He died, unnamed, the next day. Sam and Pat dug the grave on the hill southeast of the cabin. Pat carved his marker from a flat granite stone he carried from Bill Darling's place. Bessie planted irises around the grave and Pat fenced it. For years after they left the South Fork, Pat would return to mend the fence until Bessie asked to him to stop. It was her desire to let the grave and the baby return to nature.

Bessie, holding Anne

The baby's death seemed to be a turning point for the Reeds, as if it were time to leave. While Reed did not have a specific place in mind to move the family, he spent the summer of 1929 making contacts to buy cattle and to rent grazing land around Ola, northeast of Emmett. In October the family loaded the pack horses with their belongings and left the South Fork. The significance was not lost on Bessie. Later, in a letter to a great-granddaughter, she would write that they arrived and left the South Fork in "the same fashion." She would add that her days on the river were the "happiest and busiest years of my life, too busy to be unhappy or to long for things we didn't have."

The Reed Ranch did not prove bountiful for the South-Salmon Placer Mining Company. There was no gold on the ranch, and by 1945 the company was defunct. To satisfy the company's debts, the Reed Ranch was sold at a sheriff's auction to C. G. Halliday for $2,700. Halliday in turn sold the property to William Deinhard. Deinhard recognized the value of the land lay in its timber, the huge stands of Yellow Pine which covered the hillsides. In 1951 he sold the property to Brown's Tie and Lumber Company of McCall. As of this writing, the Brown family retains ownership to the land still known as the Reed Ranch.

13

Starting Over

Although Reed had studied the area around Emmett prior to the family's move from the South Fork, he was heading to no where in particular when they left. In fact, according to son Pat, his father "didn't know where he was going." But he had made arrangements for a truck to carry Bessie, the children, and their belongings from Penny Creek, where the pack trail ended on the South Fork, through High Valley and into Ola, northeast of Emmett. Reed, along with Pat, followed, trailing a few horses and some cattle into the area, leaving Sam to stay on the South Fork with the rest of the pack string. Sam would then trail the horses out the following spring.

The family stayed near Ola for only a month, living in a large wall-tent, while Reed searched for pasture land to lease. In November, the family moved into Squaw Valley, near Sweet, and leased land owned by Jim and Athena Kirkpatrick. They would remain there for the winter. Bessie became acquainted with the neighbors and tried to establish some semblance of a home for the family, including enrolling the children in school. Reed checked out the local ranches, looking for a permanent place to settle.

Reed had no trouble finding land to rent. Many of the ranchers in the Sweet area had fallen on hard times, and while the full weight of the Depression had yet to hit Idaho, many of them were already short of cash to pay their taxes or mortgages. With banks closing their doors, they had little choice but to look to individuals with money to help them out. One of those individuals was William Reed.

The family estimates Reed had $15,000 in cash when he arrived in Sweet. Wary of banks, he kept the proceeds of the South Fork sale stashed in wide mouth quart jars, which he buried wherever the family set up camp. While the money was secure most of the time, there were a few instances when Reed's unusual banking system went awry. One spring he dug up his cache, only to find his money waterlogged; he had not sufficiently sealed the jars. The children spent hours ironing the bills to get them into their original shapes. In another instance, son Penny thought he had hit a jackpot when he was exploring around an old wood shed and unearthed one of the jars. He was sorely disappointed when he found out the money belonged to his father.

Reed's banking system, while unorthodox, paid off in the end. When banks began closing their doors and people ran out of money, he had an ample supply. People soon learned that Reed had money to lend, and they came calling. He loved the attention. As his children would later recall, he felt like a "big shot" when he could help people with his money. In most cases, he just loaned people enough to catch up on their taxes taking notes against their cattle for security. But in the case of Harry Hamilton, who owned 160 acres near Sweet, Reed paid his mortgage. In the event Hamilton defaulted, Reed would get the ranch.

Reed, however, was not so adept in his other business dealings. In his desire to be a rancher, he invested a large sum of his money in cattle, buying 600 head in the spring of 1930. He leased property from Ben Newell near Montour and moved the family to the shores of Newell Lake, where son Jim was born in June 1930. Still not satisfied, however, Reed went in search of greener pastures, which he found near Harper, Oregon. He leased some land, and in July, Pat, Bill, Jr., and he drove the cattle there leav-

Nine of the twelve Reed children in the fall of 1932

ing Bessie and the children in Sweet.

The trip took ten days, and while pasture grass was plentiful at first, Reed soon became disillusioned. He and the boys had to deal with heat, dry water holes, and rattlesnakes. By late fall, he and the boys herded the cattle back to Sweet where he planned to winter them on the Hamilton ranch. From that point on, Reed remained an Idaho rancher.

For the next two years, the family wandered between ranches, unable to find a place of their own. Reed continued to lose money on his cattle investment. Shortly after he bought his herd, the price of cattle plummeted, eventually falling to ten dollars a head. Originally, he planned to sell his cattle to the big slaughterhouses in Spokane or Portland, but after his first shipment, which barely covered the cost of the rail freight, he abandoned that plan. Instead, he decided to keep his herd intact until prices recovered. According to Lafe Cox, who became acquainted with the Reeds when they lived on the South Fork, Reed made a big mistake.

"He kept a lot of those steers and fed them 'till they was eight years old," Cox said. "He kept them so long, he could only sell them for about half of what he'd give for them. He was trying to wait until the market comes up...but every time he turned around, why, he lost money."

Reed, however, was undeterred. He continued to rent ranch land around Sweet. He would winter the cattle on his leased land, and then in the spring, the entire family would load into wagons and trail the cattle north to Ola and High Valley where Reed had a government grazing lease. In the fall, he would leave Bill, Jr. and Sandy to look after the stock, while the family returned to Sweet to find a place to live for the winter. Such was the case in the winter of 1931, when the family settled into the Nielson place near Sweet. It was the first real home for the Reeds since leaving the South Fork. It featured a log cabin, good spring water, and several outbuildings. Ruth Reed was born here in April 1932.

The family remained at the Nielson homestead for the next two years. Then in April 1934, Reed decided to call in the note he was holding on Harry Hamilton's 160 acres. When Hamilton could not come up with the cash, Reed foreclosed. On April 12, Hamilton signed over his ranch to Reed, and once again, Reed became a landowner. The next month, he bought the adjoining Nielson ranch. After this transaction, he owned 680 acres, with over 200 of it in tillable farmland.

The family left the log cabin at the Nielson place and moved into the old Hamilton home. The Reed's rambling days were over.

14

Under Attack

For all the years the family lived on the South Fork, they escaped the trouble that Reed predicted would come. Save for the incident with Krassel, they lived securely in their wilderness cabin, free from threats or intrusion. The older children even began to ignore their father's warnings, believing he was just a paranoid old gunfighter trying to scare them with his stories. But in 1930 all of that changed. They no longer doubted they could be targets for Deadshot's enemies.

In the late summer of 1930, Reed, Pat, and Bill, Jr. were camped near Harper, Oregon, minding their own business and tending their newly purchased cattle. Each night, they would push the herd into the area where they had established camp, but by morning the cattle would be scattered, having worked their way up to higher ground. It was Pat's job to round up the cattle and drive them back down toward the camp.

One morning in late summer, Pat awoke to find the cattle scattered more than usual. In particular, he saw a group of steers making their way up a draw. Upon closer examination, he found they were being driven up the draw by a stranger.

Pat hurried toward the draw, traversing the rocky ground, when he was surprised by a man with a gun who rose up in front of him on the trail. The two exchanged words, and then the man pointed the gun right at Pat. Pat would later describe the gunman as "goofy." While Pat was never clear on exactly what he did next, he believed he raised his hands to show the man he was unarmed. At that point, the man shot him right through the hand. Pat could do nothing but watch the shooter and his partner get away.

Pat headed back to camp and was met by his father. Reed conjectured the men were part of a cattle rustling operation working in the area, but he was not sure. He was certain, however, that Pat was in danger. He had seen the rustlers and could identify them. Reed was sure the thieves would be back, and this time they would try to kill Pat. Not wanting to get into a shootout, he and the boys gathered the cattle and trailed them back to Sweet.

By the time the Reeds reached Idaho, the shooting was headline news, but as with most of the stories that circulated about Deadshot, this, too, became another tall tale that added to his legend.

According to an article that appeared in the Nov. 8, 1930 edition of the *Nampa Leader Herald,* Reed had been arrested and charged with the murder of Charles Murphy, a Yellow Pine rancher. The story claimed that Murphy had been grazing his cattle in Malheur County near the Reeds and accused Pat of running off some of his cattle. An argument ensued and Murphy shot Pat. On returning to Idaho, Reed refused to let the matter die and traveled to Yellow Pine where he called on Murphy. The two exchanged harsh words, and Murphy pulled his gun, only to be shot down by Reed. At the time the story was published, Reed was supposedly in the Cascade jail. The report went on to say that Reed had been with the Texas Rangers when they drove the Dalton gang out of Texas and that his injured right arm was the result of a shooting in Valley County when he was attacked by a seventeen year old boy.

The following week, the *Emmett Index* attempted to set the record straight, reporting that "Deadshot" Reed was back in Sweet, and that the sensational story, which had also appeared in the *Boise Capital News*, was "without any foundation." According to the *Index*, Reed admitted to close friend D.M. Cox that son Frank had been shot through the hand, but that he had not retaliated. Clearly, there was not a Frank Reed, but whether Cox simply forgot Pat's name when he talked to the newspaper, or whether Reed had deliberately misstated his son's name in an attempt to protect him is uncertain. It is evident, however, that Reed put his own spin on the event. The story added that Reed was "not a desperado," and that he was a "kindly dispositioned man, rather meek in appearance and demeanor, peaceable, well educated, a good neighbor, and most hospitable."

After the shooting, Reed tried to tighten the reins on his children, concerned for their safety. He became increasingly suspicious, afraid that whoever shot Pat would return to finish the job. He did not have to wait too long.

Near the end of June 1932, Pat was fishing alone near the mouth of Squaw Creek, south of Sweet. Recently completed Highway 52 ran close by. Pat was about to make another cast when a man with a rifle suddenly appeared on the bank above him. According to Pat, the man aimed his rifle and then claimed "I got you now." Pat drew his .38 revolver that he had tucked in his belt, but before he could respond, the man shot. A single bullet creased Pat's chest just above his heart, and he fell back into the creek. By the time he made his way up to the road, the man was gone.

Bleeding profusely, Pat was sitting at the side of the road when he was found by Game Warden Bill Talley. Talley drove Pat home, and then notified the Gem County Sheriff. For his part, Reed took his gun and for the rest of the night stopped every car that passed along the highway, looking for his son's attacker.

Pat refused to talk about the incident with investigators, but privately admitted to his father that the shooter was the same man who had attacked him in Oregon. Reed vowed to catch him, and for the next several months, Pat and he traveled to various cattle sales, looking for the assailant. They always went armed, as Reed was determined to put an end to the problem. However, they were never able to find the shooter.

All of the Reeds were convinced that Pat was in danger. The longer he stayed in the Sweet area, the greater his risk. Pat never cared for the ranching business anyway, and he particularly disliked the dry scrub brush around Sweet. As he put it, he "never had no use for that country." Later that summer, he left home and traveled back to the South Fork to start a life of his own.

Pat left home in 1933. Shortly after his departure, Reed's life was also threatened. He was riding by himself along Canal Road near Sweet, looking for loose cattle, when a car pulled alongside of him. Thinking it was a neighbor, Reed reined his horse, but the horse resisted. As he tried to control the animal, the car passed, and a man in the back seat rose up and took a shot at Reed. The car then sped off, but not before Reed got off a few good shots of his own, shattering the back window of the car. He chased the car on horseback for a quarter mile before he gave up. On his return home, Reed reported the incident to the Gem County Sheriff, giving him a description of the car and the shooter. Later the car was found in Jordan Valley, Oregon. Bullet holes and blood were found in both the front and back seats of the car. The owner, a man named Davis, was never found.

Reed was convinced that all the shootings were related, but he could never determine who was responsible. The incidents made him all the more wary of strangers and fed the paranoia that enveloped him in his later years. For the remainder of his days in Sweet, he carried a gun, supposedly with the permission of the Gem County sheriff. At night when he went to bed, it hung over his bedpost. When he camped out with his cattle, he slept with it under his pillow. All of these precautions, however, were unnecessary. Reed was never challenged to pull his gun again.

15

Settling in Sweet

The move into the old Hamilton house in the spring of 1934 was a blessing to Bessie and the rest of the family. With a place to call their own, they could settle into the type of family life they had known on the South Fork. Their new home was no mansion, but the boys worked on it until it met their needs.

When the Reeds arrived, the house had but two rooms, a living room and a bedroom. They immediately added a 12′ x 20′ kitchen that held a large wood cookstove with warming ovens and a water boiler. Cabinets, with heavy-duty bins for storing flour and sugar, lined its walls. For their meals, the entire family sat around an oblong table built by Reed and the boys. The living room was smaller, just 12′ x 14′. A wood heater sat in the middle of the room while a double bed stood in one corner. The bed belonged to Bessie and Reed and was made up first thing every morning. The children were never allowed to sit on the bed, even if someone needed a seat; the floor, made of pine plank, would have to do. Other furniture included a library table and three wooden chairs. Eventually, the family purchased a wind-up Victrola and a matching couch and chair. The bedroom was more of a lean-to, added to the house. It held two beds, two dressers, and a closet. The youngest children slept here, while the rest of the children slept outside in tents or in the granary, except in the coldest of weather when the girls would share the room. Eventually, as the older children moved out, Ruth claimed this bedroom for her own.

The children pose near Sweet. From left, Ruth, Marge, Jim, Anne, and Nora. Notice Anne and Nora's high top shoes.

The boys also added a front porch to the house. The 8′ x 12′ room held a cot, where Reed would rest during the day. The cream separator also sat on the front porch, and in later years, Bessie kept her gas-fired washing machine there as well.

Bessie was meticulous in her new house. She kept it spotless, especially her floors, which she scrubbed and varnished regularly. Outside the front door on the wooden walkway, Reed had placed a raised metal strip where the children were to scrape their boots. According to Ruth, it was "bad news if you were caught coming into the living room with dirty shoes." Bessie kept up the regimen of family meals which she had started years earlier on the South Fork. The table was always prepared with a clean table cloth and correct place settings, and when the family sat down to eat, the children were expected to use proper manners. As for the laundry, Bessie continued to use her washboard and tubs, hanging the clothes on a line outside the house. Her children remember that she was always clean and neat, and she tried her best to keep them the same way. She insisted that each child wash every day, and on Saturday she supervised their weekly baths, complete with hot water and a full scrubbing in a big, round washtub.

Besides the farmhouse, the Hamilton place had several outbuildings, including a large two-story barn, a tack shed, and a granary. The barn held stalls for the horses and stanchions for the milk cows, while the tack shed featured a wooden rail on which the children were to hang their saddles. Reed was very particular about how the children took care of their gear for the horses. If he went into the tack shed and found anything on the ground or a saddle awry, the child at fault would be fully punished. As for the granary, it served a dual purpose; the family turned it into a bunkhouse so it not only stored grain, but children as well.

In addition, the family had two wells, one near the house and the other in the barnyard, both with pitcher pumps. The well near the house was also used as the refrigerator. Bessie had a large bucket attached to a rope. She would put the day's milk and butter into the bucket and then lower it into the well to keep it cool. Near the house, she also had a large root cellar where she kept all of the family's canned goods, barrel pickles, and winter vegetables. In the heat of the summer, it became a favorite place for Bessie and the children. She kept some of her books there, and on the hot summer days in July and August, she would take the children into the cellar and read to them.

The area around the house, cellar, and well was set off with a five-wire barbed fence. Bessie kept a small patch of grass next to the house, using her wash water to keep it green. She also had a lilac bush and several yellow rose bushes which the children had to water. She and her family were well settled when she gave birth to her fourteenth child.

Floyd Reed was born October 18, 1934, at home. While he thrived at first, during the last week of October he became ill. He died November 7, probably of pneumonia, and was buried on the ranch. He would be the last of the Reed children.

When the family finally settled in at the Hamilton place, William Reed was getting along in years. At 58, he relied heavily on the boys to get most of the work done. With Sam and Pat on their own, the work fell to Bill and Sandy. In their teens, they did the work of grown men—putting up hay in the summer and fall, taking care of the horses, driving the cattle to their summer range in High Valley. They mended fence, shod the horses, and brought in the grain crops in the late summer. Around the house, they kept the wood box full and the buildings in good repair. They did all of this work under the watchful eye of their father, who most of the time was impossible to please but did little to help.

The girls continued to help their mother as they had on the South Fork. Although Mabel was in her early twenties, she was still at home when the family moved into the Hamilton's house. Mabel, Rose, and Marge performed many of the duties around the house, making bread, washing clothes, tending to the garden, and preparing meals. They also looked after the younger children until they were big enough to care for themselves.

The girls also were in charge of the milk cows, which not only provided food for the family but also extra income. Under the direction of Rose, the girls milked the cows each morning and night. They would then separate the cream and sell both the cream and the whole milk to the creamery. They had to carry the large milk cans down to the main road, about an eighth of a mile, where the creamery truck would pick them up. What milk

Jim and Ruth on the day of Floyd's funeral

the girls did not sell, they would turn into butter, cheese, and cottage cheese for the family. The girls also brought in extra income by selling eggs and taking in laundry from the neighbors.

The family needed the extra money. Unlike on the South Fork where Reed could make a living trapping and packing, in Sweet he had to make an income from his ranch. He was not successful. The price of cattle did not recover, and the family struggled financially. What they did have had to be saved to pay taxes, grazing fees, and necessities for the ranch. Reed refused to spend any money on items that would make life easier for his wife and children. As a result, Bessie learned to make do with what little she had, but for the children that was sometimes hard to understand. For the first time, they were interacting with others; they were exposed to the outside world, and they were all eager to participate.

Attending school on a regular basis was a new experience for the Reed children, but for Bessie it was important that the children receive an education. Each morning after their chores, she would send them on their way, a two mile walk to the school house. The girls excelled in school, especially Marge and Anne who graduated from the eighth grade at the head of their respective classes. Ruth also earned co-valedictorian honors with her best friend Mary Anna Kirkpatrick. The boys, however, did not place the stock in school that the girls did. Convinced by their father that education was not important, they were known to play hooky on more than one occasion. According to Pat, Bill, Sandy, and Penny would spend much of their time in the hills around Sweet visiting with old moonshiners they had met while running cattle in the area.

At school, the children were well accepted by their classmates and made many friends. Of course, they were a formidable group. No one ever picked on a Reed without facing retribution from every Reed on the playground. This was especially true in the case of Penn, who had difficulty in school. If anyone made fun of him or called him names, the rest of his family—especially Margaret, Anne, and Nora—stuck up for him.

While the children fought typical childhood battles on the playground, no one ever gave them a hard time about having Deadshot Reed for a father. In fact, among the children, it never came up. According to Ruth, the only people who seemed concerned about them were the adults they met, who would often drop by the house just to see Deadshot.

Education for most of the children ended after the eighth grade; no matter how well they did in school or how much they begged to go on, Reed forbade them. He would not even listen

Bessie and William Reed. When this picture was taken, Bessie was angry at Reed because he refused to take off his hat.

to Bessie on this issue. The only exceptions were Jim and Ruth; by the time they entered high school, Reed was too old and powerless to stop them. Pat, however, later recalled that his father really "climbed the walls," when they went on to high school.

If Reed railed against education, he was equally as adamant against religion. While Bessie had read the Bible to the children on the South Fork, she had to do it when Reed was not around. According to Marge, the only religious training she received on the river was the swearing that came from her father. Reed wanted nothing to do with religion, even threatening to shoot the Victrola one evening when someone tried to play the record "Get in Touch with God, Turn your Radio On." But the more time the children, especially the girls, spent around other people, the more they realized that something was missing from their lives. They were invited to church meetings and picnics, but Reed steadfastly refused his permission, which embarrassed

Pictured, from left, are Pat, Sam, Reed, Sandy, Bill, Penn, and Jim. In front of Pat is his son David.

Bessie. While the boys eventually bought into his way of thinking, the girls refused to give up. They were curious and determined to find out about religion.

The girls—Mabel, Marge, and Rose—had their first taste of organized religion at a tent revival meeting in Sweet. While Reed first told them they could not attend, he finally relented on one condition: the boys would have to take them. Because he knew his sons shared his views, he believed there was no chance the girls would end up at the revival.

The girls were undaunted. At first the boys were opposed to the idea, but then the sisters tried some home-made blackmail. If the boys did not take them to the revival, they would get no more fresh pies or cakes, and they would have to wash their own Levis. The boys—Pat, who was home visiting, Sandy, and Bill—had no choice but to deliver the girls to the revival. They hitched up the family's buggy and drove the girls to Sweet.

Mabel, Marge, and Rose were completely inexperienced; they had no idea what went on at a revival. The boys, older and wiser, warned them and gave them explicit instructions to sit in the back row. Under no circumstances were they to get up and go forward with the congregation. If they did, the brothers threatened, they would cut the ropes of the tent. The girls agreed to remain seated, but they were overwhelmed by the sermons and the singing. In the middle of the service, they stood up and went forward to accept the Lord. The boys, true to their word, cut the tent ropes, and the canvas came down.

Reed, of course, was livid when he heard what happened. While he was proud of the actions of the boys, he was disgusted with his three oldest daughters. They were forever forbidden to attend a church service or meeting. Unfortunately for Deadshot, his children were tired of following his unreasonable rules. In time they learned that the rules were meant to be broken.

Pictured, from left, are Bessie, Mabel, Rose, Anne, Marge, and Nora. Ruth is in the front.

16

Losing control

Those who knew Reed understood one thing for sure; no matter what the situation, he had to be in charge. Egotistical and domineering, he would get control using any means possible, whether it be turning on his irresistible charm, threatening an enemy, or intimidating his children. Only Bessie had any influence over him.

Reed and Bessie clearly loved one another. According to daughter Ruth, the two constantly gave each other little love pats and hugs, even in front of the children. Reed was always polite and respectful to Bessie, particularly when it came to matters around the house. For that reason, she was sometimes able to persuade her husband to loosen the restrictions on the children, especially after they moved to Sweet. Most of the time, however, Reed refused to relinquish his authority. It was this domineering control coupled with his cruelty that eventually drove the children away.

By the time the family settled in Sweet, Bill, Sandy, and Penn were teenagers. After being isolated on the South Fork for so long, they suddenly had an opportunity to explore new things. They wanted to chase girls, drive cars, and go to work in the local sawmills. Reed, however, had other ideas. He needed and expected the boys to work on the farm and to take care of the stock. He even tempted them with money, offering them the proceeds from the sale of the cattle. Of course, when the cattle market collapsed, Reed had no money to give them. He took his frustrations out on the boys.

Penn was often a victim of his outbursts, more so than the other boys. It did not help that he often argued with the old man. Even when he did try to please his father, it was never good enough. In one particular instance, right after they moved into the Hamilton place, the brothers were rounding up cattle. Penn was in charge of counting them, but when Reed approached and asked him for the count, he was unsure of the number. Reed erupted, took his revolver, and hit Penn across the forehead with the butt of the gun. He fell from his horse and lay on the ground as his father rode away. When he recovered, he walked back to the house and told his mother what had happened. That day he left home; he never lived under Reed's roof again.

While Reed never hit the girls, except for an occasional spanking, he denied them any pleasure. Whenever he could, he found excuses to keep them from school. They were never allowed to go to church or to visit friends. According to daughter Anne, his favorite word was "no." They could not wear makeup or even lipstick. They could not date. God help the boy who wanted to date a daughter of Deadshot Reed.

But the more rules he placed on them, the more they rebelled. The more they rebelled, the more freedom they experienced. Eventually they learned not to ask his permission for anything, because it only caused a fight. Instead, they began to do whatever they pleased, which was easy when they were all sleeping in the bunk house. They would wait until their parents were in bed, then walk the horses down to the main road. From there they would ride off to Grange Hall dances, church meetings, or any other activities that suited their fancy. In all the times they sneaked away, they were never caught.

While the children learned to deal with Reed's unreasonable restrictions, they had a more difficult time dealing with his cruelty. He was unpredictable: congenial one minute and homicidal the next. Both Anne and Ruth described him as having a split personality. While he could entertain them for hours with his stories and card tricks, he could terrorize them in an instant if something went wrong. All of them had stared down the barrel of his gun on more than one occasion. They learned early not to violate his rules, but often, they did not know what the rules were.

The children knew that the cattle and horses were important to Reed. Water troughs had to be kept full all the time, and the horses could never be ridden hard. But Reed took this to an extreme. Early one summer, Reed was out moving cattle for several weeks. Rose got the idea that she wanted to plant a garden with both flowers and vegetables for the family. She dug the ground herself, planted the seeds, and diverted water to the garden from the barnyard well. When Reed returned and found that water for his precious cattle had been diverted to Rose's garden, he went into a tirade. He walked through the garden kicking and screaming and then refused to let Rose use any more water. The garden, in the heat of Sweet's summer, died.

To the children, it seemed that Reed wanted to deny them every pleasure. If they had something they enjoyed, he tried to ruin it for them. He was very hard on the children's pets, showing no sympathy in the event that one of them was injured or died. The children were convinced that he cared only about his own needs.

When Ruth was seven, she had a large gray cat that she loved dearly. They were inseparable and the cat would sit on her lap and wrap its paws around her neck. This irritated her father, but Ruth ignored him and continued to shower the cat with affection. One evening after the cows had been milked and the cream separated, the girls poured the foam into a large pan for the animals. Sitting on the porch, they watched as Ruth's cat

Nora and Anne at their home in Sweet. As children, they were inseparable

and Reed's new Australian shepherd puppy raced for the treat. The cat, older and stronger, would not let the pup drink. Reed, infuriated, threatened to shoot the cat. When Ruth protested, he pulled out his gun and shot it. He then carried it out and threw it into the pasture.

Ruth was both distraught and angry. All night long she thought of killing her father with his own gun; only the threat of jail stopped her. The next morning, her anger turned to disbelief and then disgust when she saw her cat on the porch. According to her father, the bullet had just grazed the cat. When he had thrown it into the field, it ran away. He just never bothered to tell her.

Anne, Rose, and Nora also wanted to kill their father at various times. They would lie in bed at night and discuss the different methods they could use without getting caught. Of course, they never followed through with their plans, although Nora one time came close. Of the girls, Nora was the most outspoken. She was not afraid to confront Reed, even if he was in one of his unreasonable moods.

Reed was quick to anger if the children did not follow his orders, even if they tried. These tirades often occurred when the children were caring for the cattle and horses, who had minds of their own. On one occasion, Reed told Jim and Anne to ride out and bring in the horses that were on the hill behind the house. He specifically told them not to run the horses as they brought them in. Anne and Jim did what they were told. They slowly gathered the horses together, got behind them, and started moving them toward the barn. The horses, however, sensing they were going to be fed, started to run. Reed watched as they went into a full gallop, his children helpless to stop them. Livid, he grabbed a quirt, a riding whip, from where it hung on the house and headed out to meet Anne and Jim. He told Nora and Ruth, who were also watching, that he was going to "get them good with this quirt."

Nora spoke up in her siblings' defense, telling her father that if he hit Jim and Anne, she would hit him. Reed looked at her in disgust, told her to go away, and then headed toward the barnyard. Nora, true to her word, grabbed a whip with a long, hard handle and followed her father.

Reed met Jim and Anne at the gate, his whip extended and ready. When his son tried to plead his case, claiming the horses ran on their own, Reed wrapped the whip around Jim's waist and pulled him from the horse. As he raised the whip to strike him, Nora smacked her father behind the head with the handle of her whip. To the surprise of everyone, Nora knocked him out. Realizing she was in much trouble, she ran for the house, grabbed a few belongings, and went to stay with neighbors for a few weeks. When she returned home, her father never said a word to her. News of Nora's pluck had spread to Sweet and according to Ruth, her father knew "it was best to drop the matter." Shortly after, at age fourteen, Nora left home.

This was to be the case with most of the children. They could deal with their father for just so long before he drove them away. While he provided for them and taught them many survival skills they would use over the years, he could not stop himself from mistreating them. Only Jim and Ruth had an easier time with him. By the time they were in their teens, Reed was too old even to try to control them. Although he sometimes threatened to send Ruth to reform school, she would just banter back, daring him to do so. But for the middle children—Anne, Rose, Marge, Nora, and Penn—life with Reed was torment. They resented their father long into their adult years.

17

Deadshot's Decline

By the early 1940s, only Jim and Ruth remained at the home in Sweet. The work of the farm fell on their shoulders, as well as on their mother. Reed, in his mid-to-late sixties, was too old to be of much help.

With his age, however, came freedom for his family. While Jim and Ruth had chores to do before and after school, they also enjoyed activities unknown to their older brothers and sisters. They freely attended church, school activities, and Grange Hall dances. They entered local rodeos at Ola and Horseshoe Bend, with Ruth excelling in the barrel races and Jim roping steers and riding bulls. Both of them enrolled in high school, and Jim played football for the Montour High School team.

While Reed had purchased an old truck when the family moved to Sweet, neither he nor Bessie ever learned to drive. He did make two attempts, but all he ever managed to do was destroy an entire line of fence posts on one occasion, and drive straight into a tree in the other. In the tree incident, Mabel and Rose were along for the ride, and Rose was thrown from the truck. After that, no one would ride with him, and he gave up, leaving the driving to his older sons. Both Pat and Sam had cars shortly after leaving home. When they came to visit, they would gladly teach the younger children to drive. Sam was almost too patient with the girls, giving them instructions many times over, even after the girls had mastered the concepts.

Pat helped his mother achieve a life-long dream. In the late

Sam was missing from this picture of Reed and his sons. From left are Reed, Bill, Penn, Pat, Sandy, and Jim.

1930s, he drove his mother and Anne north to Peck, Idaho, where Bessie reunited with her mother, Mary Warren. Mary welcomed Bessie back into the family, and she was able to visit with her brothers and sisters. Bessie would make several more visits and many of the Reed children would meet their grandmother before her death in 1943.

Bessie also began to venture outside the home. She attended church in Sweet and became involved in its social functions. Then in 1944, she went to work. She not only could use the income but also was concerned about her future. She wanted to earn credit with Social Security so that when she was older, she could draw a pension.

At first, Bessie went to work cooking and cleaning at the Roystone Hot Springs near Sweet. The popular resort featured a boarding house and therapeutic pools and massage. Bessie would stay at the springs during the week, returning to the farm on the weekends. Eventually, she left the resort and went to work at the fruit packing plant in Emmett. Since that job was seasonal, she hired on as a cook for a logging camp, where she joined three of her sons. Eventually, she returned to the Emmett area where she was employed by different families to cook and clean.

While Bessie worked, Jim and Ruth were left to take care of the farm and their father. Only fourteen and twelve, respectively, they did all their morning chores, went to school, and then returned home to more work. Ruth also did all the household chores including the cooking and laundry. It was a sad day for Ruth when Jim left home in 1946, leaving her with all the work and an increasingly cantankerous father.

Life was a struggle. The farm did not make much of an income, and the work was hard. Bessie worried about paying the bills and providing for her family, which for a short time included Pat's two sons, Dave and Don. The older children, however, all pitched in to help. With the boys making a steady income either logging or working for the Forest Service, they first purchased Bessie a gas-fired washing machine to replace her wash board. In 1947, they signed a contract with Idaho Power to run a line to the house, something their father had refused to do. For the first time, Bessie had a refrigerator. Ruth was still at home then, and she and Bessie gladly gave up the old bucket that hung in the well.

From time to time, various children returned to live at or near the farm in Sweet. Bill married and moved into the Nielson place in the late 1930s. He took charge of the daily operations of the farm and was truly a lifesaver for Bessie. Sandy returned for a short time and took up residency in the granary with his wife and children. Rose stayed with her mother the longest, helping with Pat's children before leaving to be with her fiancé, Everett Swander, whose family owned the farm adjacent to the Reed's.

Jim, on leave from the service, stands with his parents at the ranch in Sweet. The picture was taken in 1952.

Swander fought in World War II and, when he was discharged, he and Rose returned to Sweet to farm.

The other girls were long gone, following husbands to different parts of the country. Ruth was the last daughter to leave, eloping in 1949. Reed, who continued to wear his gun every day, threatened to shoot her new husband. Fortunately, Bessie intervened, reminding him of the trouble they faced when they had eloped. When Ruth brought her husband Bill Beckett home to meet her father, Reed treated him well. He told Beckett his stories of the Wild West and showed him his quick draw. More than once, Beckett would turn to find Reed's gun pointing at him. As a precautionary measure and without Reed's knowledge, Jim removed the firing pin.

Jim returned home in the early 1950s to look out for his par-

William Reed
with one of
his grandsons

ents. Then he joined the Marines and did a tour of duty in Korea. He sent his pay home to his mother, which Bessie put to good use. Among other neccessities, she purchased an electric pump for the well in the barn lot. No longer did she have to fill the large stone watering trough by hand. Without Jim's financial assistance, his parents would not have survived. When he returned to Emmett following his service, he continued to help.

Into the 1950s, Bessie took various jobs, while Reed's health continued to decline. Reed must have sensed the end was near because one Sunday morning he put on his best shirt, walked to Sweet, and went to church. Following the service, he approached

Pat with his two sons David and Don who lived with their grandparents in the 1940s

the minister and asked if he could be saved. He was later baptized. According to Bessie, Reed was forever a changed man. He enjoyed having his children visit and was especially gentle with his grandchildren. Still, however, he suffered from bouts of depression and unpredictable behavior.

In 1954, Bessie was milking three cows twice a day, selling eggs, taking care of her husband, and working at the packing plant in Emmett. Each morning after chores, she would walk two miles to Sweet, where she hitched a ride to the plant. She would return home in the evening to more chores and then fall exhausted into bed.

The hard work finally caught up with her. One night in September, Bessie awoke to a crushing pain in her chest, a heart attack. At first, Reed told her she was fine, but when the pain did not subside, she insisted that he go for help. Disoriented and frightened, Reed was unsure of what to do. Rather than walk to the Swander's farm, directly adjacent to his place where there was a phone, Reed walked towards Sweet. He made his way to the home of Art Eldridge, who in turn called for an ambulance. Eventually, Bessie was rushed to the hospital where she remained in intensive care for several weeks.

At the time, Ruth and Bill were living in San Diego with their new daughter. When they heard of Bessie's heart attack, Bill pulled the couple's new travel trailer to Idaho and set it up next to the family home. Bill had to return to duty with the Navy, but Ruth remained. She moved Bessie into the trailer so she could take better care of her. Jim, now married, had an apartment in Emmett, but he moved back into the family home and took over the operation of the farm. According to Ruth, Bessie was easy, a true "joy" who was grateful the children were there to help. Reed, on the other hand, was a handful. He refused to let Ruth help him, instead demanding that Bessie get out of bed and take care of him. He was also hard on Jim. Although Reed was not capable of doing any work on the farm himself, he refused to relinquish control, constantly criticizing Jim's handling of the cattle and horses.

The conflict became a crisis on Thanksgiving. The family was planning a feast and Bessie, Ruth, and Shirley, Jim's wife, were busy in the kitchen. Jim and his father had walked to the barn to milk and do morning chores. When they had finished milking, Reed opened the gate so the cows could go into the pasture, but Jim stopped him. He told his dad he wanted to keep the stock in so he would not have to track them down in the evening. That way he would have more time to spend visiting with his brothers and sisters. The two argued, but Jim held his ground. He fed the cows some hay, and then he and his father walked back to the house.

Jim made himself comfortable in the living room while Reed

The Reed family—only two sons are missing. Front row, left to right, Anne, Ruth, Reed, Bessie, Mabel, and Nora. Back row, Marge, Sam, Pat, Sandy, and Rose.

entered the kitchen. He was still fuming because his son had disagreed with him. He opened a kitchen drawer and took out a large butcher knife that he then hid behind his back. Shirley watched the scene unfold. As Reed walked slowly into the living room toward his youngest son, Shirley yelled, "He has a knife!" As Jim stood up and approached his father, Reed raised the knife. He brought it down and Jim grabbed it, cutting his palm. Jim then hit his father, knocking him back and taking the knife from his hand.

Reed had finally stepped over the line. His attack on Jim proved that with his depression and senility, no one was safe. There was no guarantee that he would not lash out again and harm someone else, perhaps another son or a grandchild, perhaps even Bessie.

Immediately after the incident, Jim, Ruth, and Sandy, who

arrived shortly after the attack, put Reed in Jim's car and drove to Emmett where they met with the sheriff. The sheriff agreed to place Reed in custody and locked him in the Gem County jail. Reed went willingly, seeming to realize that he had done something wrong. Jim then visited a doctor who stitched up his hand. The doctor advised the family that they had few options in dealing with their father. He could be placed in a nursing home, which the family could not afford, or they could commit him to the State Mental Hospital at Blackfoot. While the choice was obvious, it was a difficult one to make.

Not everyone in the family agreed with having Reed institutionalized, but no one wanted to take him. On the Monday following Thanksgiving, Jim, Ruth, Shirley, and grandson Don drove Reed to Blackfoot where he was committed.

The family visited Reed several times during his stay. According to Ruth, sometimes he knew them, sometimes he did not. On occassion he did not recognize Bessie. Still, he knew he did not belong in Blackfoot. In August 1955, Reed told a nurse that all he wanted was "someone to take him home."

Reed spent the rest of his life in the state hospital. He died May 31, 1958. Over 200 people attended his funeral in Emmett, many of them complete strangers who just wanted to get a look at Deadshot Reed.

18

Bessie's Peace

William Reed had been a part of Bessie's life since she was fourteen. To be suddenly without him was devastating. He had been the only love of her life and, once he was gone, she missed him terribly.

Bessie, 1962

The children often questioned why she had stayed with him all those years, putting up with his temper, following him from place to place with his wild ideas of being a rancher, listening to the rumors that were repeated and embellished. But Bessie was unwavering in her devotion to him. The handsome Texan had swept her off her feet when she was just a child, and those feelings for him remained with her until the day she died. According to Anne, "Mom loved him. She never wanted to replace him or never wanted to leave him." When granddaughter Alberta Smith asked her why she never remarried after Reed's death, she replied, "I had the very best, and I knew I couldn't settle for anything else." When the children spoke badly of their father, Bessie would let them, but then she would defend him. She would remind them that there was not one time in their lives when they did not have food to eat or clothes to wear. They had stayed together as a family for forty-eight years, and although she was the strength and heart of the family, she gave him credit for being a great provider. The children would have to agree that in spite of his horrible temper, he had always taken care of their basic physical needs.

Their emotional needs were something else. Their feelings for Reed were based on fear and intimidation, not love and respect. Many of them would struggle with those feelings long after they left home. But their feelings for Bessie ran strong and deep. The children remember her as kind, warm, and loving, "altogether different from what Dad was," according to Pat. She freely offered the children hugs and encouragement, safety and compassion. She was proud of all of them and wanted them to be proud of who they were.

For those reasons, Bessie resisted anyone who wanted to capitalize on her husband's infamous reputation. On three occasions, she was approached by writers who wanted permission to tell Reed's life story. She refused. In a letter to one, Earl Willson, she wrote "I have no desire to be embarrassed or have the family endure any more notoriety." Bessie wanted Reed to be remembered as the good man that she knew and loved. She was also afraid Reed's enemies would continue to haunt her children. She wanted all of her children and herself to live the rest of their days in peace.

Bessie voiced only one regret about her life, and that dealt with the education of her children. In a letter addressed to all of them, she wrote that she enjoyed "every minute" of rearing them, but if she had her years to live over she would have "struggled harder than I did in regards to your education."

The last days of her life were peaceful, although at first very difficult. Following Reed's hospitalization, she went to live with

Bessie on the farm at Sweet with the family pets

daughter Ruth in San Diego for a short time. When Ruth's husband was discharged from the Navy, they returned to Sweet and the farm, but it was not profitable. Eventually, in 1957, Bessie sold the place for $5,000 and bought a small house in Emmett.

Because she could not draw Social Security until 1959, her financial situation was desperate. Money was so tight that when Reed died, Bessie had to use an installment plan to pay for his funeral. Her children did all they could to help as Rose, Anne, Nora, and Ruth all sent her twenty dollars a month to help pay the bills. The boys kept her freezer full of elk and venison from their hunting trips, and Rose provided fresh fruit and vegetables from her garden in the summer.

In the early 1960s, her circumstances suddenly improved when she received an inheritance of $65,000 from her aunt Lucy McQuesten of Boston, sister of Aaron Warren. The gift came as quite a surprise and a relief to Bessie. With the financial freedom, Bessie began to travel, visiting her children and grandchildren. She bought her grandchildren gifts which she could not afford before, even though her children urged her to spend the money on herself. She spent much of her time with Ruth, who in 1960 had moved to Tennessee with her family. Ruth enjoyed her mother's company so much, she once persuaded her to stay for three years.

Always an avid reader, Bessie finally had time in her later years to enjoy the books she loved. She followed politics and could talk to anyone about the issues of the day. She taught herself to play the piano and enjoyed playing the hymns she heard at church, which she attended every Sunday. She opened her doors to all of her grandchildren, and over the years her home became a safe haven. From broken romances to unruly children, they came to ask for her advice. No one was ever turned away.

In early 1976, Bessie was in Tennessee with Ruth when she decided to return home to Emmett. She told her youngest daughter she needed "to get her affairs in order." Daughters Marge

The Reed children, from left: Sam, Nora, Rose, Penn, Pat, Ruth, Jim, Bill, Sandy, Mabel, Marge, and Anne.

and Mabel arrived in Emmett to help. Marge later said that Bessie kept her busy those last few months, cleaning and painting. Just as she had all of her life, Bessie wanted everything to be neat and tidy when it was time for her to go.

In late July 1976, Bessie was admitted to the Emmett hospital. She died two weeks later on August 8 of heart failure. She was buried next to her beloved husband in the Sweet-Montour Cemetery.

19

Epilogue: The Children

While stories of Deadshot Reed frequently surface in the tales of Pierce, the South Fork, and Sweet, his legacy really is his children. They were a determined lot, who wanted nothing more than to live honest, decent lives. Although they were very different from one another, they all got along. No matter how difficult their lives were, they pitched in to help each other and, more importantly, their mother. If there was one thing they did have in common, it was an undying desire to make her life better.

Each child took a different road in life, although the boys, were never far away from the hunting and fishing they learned to love as children. The girls followed their husbands to all parts of the country, just as their mother had followed their father. Each one, however, grew up proud to be a Reed.

Samuel Oliver Reed

Of all the children, Sam seemed most affected by his early life on the South Fork. A kind, gentle man who loved animals, he was also described as "slow" by some of his siblings. He went to work for the Forest Service in 1928 and over the years did odd jobs for them, especially during fire season. Sam knew the South Fork better than anyone else, and because of this knowledge, he was invaluable to the Forest Service. Sam also worked as a sheepherder for such sheepmen as Little and Cruickshank. He was well known throughout Valley and Gem counties for his herding skills.

Sam Reed

His dedication to his job almost cost him his life. In the early 1940s, he was in the high country with a band of sheep when he suffered an appendicitis attack. Rather than leave the sheep and go for help, Sam trailed them for four days, turning them over to another herder before he sought help for himself. By the time he made it to the hospital, his appendix had ruptured. He spent several weeks recovering in intensive care.

Sam loved to eat. He would often arrive at his mother's home at dinnertime and stay long enough to get his clothes washed. On holidays, after his mother was gone, Sam would visit his sisters and brothers, moving from house to house, sometimes getting as many as three Christmas or Thanksgiving feasts in one day. Other times, when he needed the company, he would show up at a sister's house and visit, living in a camper on the back of his truck.

Sam was small in stature but strong. He was an excellent hunter and always made sure his sisters had an ample supply of fresh elk or venison. He was extremely kind to all of his brothers and sisters; if they needed something, he always tried to get it for them.

Sam never married. He spent much of his later life near Emmett where he and Penn owned a small ranch. In the late 1980s, Sam moved into the rest home in Emmett where Penn visited him each day. Sam died there in May 1990.

Mabel Reed Davis

As the oldest daughter, Mabel was called on to help with the smaller children. While her brothers and sisters remember her as "bossy," they had a great deal of respect for all the responsibility she had to bear. Keeping track of all the young Reed children was Mabel's job, and it was not an easy task.

Born in Canada, Mabel spent the first two years of her life in a wagon as her parents looked for a place to settle permanently. Mabel was three when the family moved into the South Fork cabin.

Of all the girls, Mabel was the most shy. She was seventeen years old when the family moved from the South Fork; she never really learned to feel comfortable around new people. According to her nieces, she seemed extremely self-conscience and preferred to surround herself with her family. She also had a soft spot in her heart for all animals, which often put her at odds with her father. She could not tolerate her father's behavior, and they argued often.

Once in Sweet, Mabel joined the Assembly of God Church, and over the years became extremely religious. She met Warren Davis at a church meeting, and they were married in 1936. The couple moved to Washington state and then Warren joined the army during World War II. He was sent first to California and then Florida; Mabel followed him. When he was shipped overseas, Mabel stayed in Tampa, where she went to work in a rubber factory.

Following the war, they tried their luck in Missouri and California before returning to Idaho, where they both went to work at Stibnite, near present day Yellow Pine. Mabel was an excellent cook and, when she needed work, that is what she did. She had learned much about cooking for a large group by taking care of all her brothers and sisters.

When the Stibnite area was abandoned, Warren and Mabel returned to Missouri where they found work and remained until they retired. They had no children of their own but adopted two children, Ruth and David.

Although Mabel was shy, she was daring. She thought nothing of driving by herself across the country to visit her family. This started when Warren was in the service and continued after the couple moved to Missouri.

In the spring of 1976, Mabel returned to Emmett with her children to take care of her mother. Warren joined her soon after, and they remained in Emmett for the rest of their lives. She died in 1984.

David Patrick Reed

Pat's real name was David Patrick, although he was always called Pat. Of all the children he had the best relationship with his father. He knew and understood his father's temper, choosing to keep his mouth shut and stay out of his way. "That's the only way to get along with anybody like that—quick tempered, you know," Pat once said. "You just gotta let them have their own way."

Raised on the South Fork, Pat became an excellent hunter and trapper. He was respected for his abilities, and sheep ranchers as well as the Idaho Fish and Game would seek his help in hunting down problem animals. He was well known for his talent in hunting cougar. He once estimated that he had taken over 400 cougars from Central Idaho. He made his living as a trapper, hunter, and guide most of his life.

After the shooting incidents in Harper and Sweet, Pat returned to the South Fork. Both he and his father thought he would be safe there, but that was not the case. While boarding at the Willey Ranch and working for the Forest Service, Pat was forced to defend himself.

Pat was lying in his bunk at the ranch when a man named Mike Popovich, an old moon shiner who spoke with a heavy accent, entered the bunk house. Drunk, Popovich demanded Pat get out of bed and drink with him. Pat refused. Angry, Popovich grabbed a double-bit ax that sat by the stove and threatened to kill Pat. Pat thought the old man was going to hit him with it, but instead he threw it. Pat rolled and the ax landed square in his pillow. With that, Pat pulled his .38 and shot three

Pat and his pet bobcats

times. He then walked over to the Willey cabin and told the people there what had happened. Sim Willey called out to Cascade, and the next day the sheriff, a doctor, and the prosecuting attorney arrived at the ranch. Popovich was still alive, so they made a travois and took him out by trail to the nearest road. From there he was taken to Cascade, then to Boise where he died. Before he died, Popovich told the prosecuting attorney that he had been sent to kill Pat. After an inquest, the court concluded Pat had shot in self-defense. After the Popovich incident, there would be no more attempts on Pat's life.

Pat married Hazel Shirrell in 1935 and, for a short time, they stayed with his parents. They had two sons, Dave and Don, and then divorced. In the late 1940s, he remarried, and his new wife Zoe Fisher shared his interests. Zoe went everywhere with him, helping him trap and hunt. When Pat started his guide business, Zoe was his cook. They stayed in the back country near Yellow Pine until Pat retired. They then moved to the Boise area. Pat and Zoe had three children, Coral, George, and Daryl.

In the summer of 1990, Pat and several of his brothers and sisters gathered at the old Reed Ranch on the South Fork. Pat's memories of the time he spent on the river were very clear and he told many stories of his family's life. He died in June 2000 and is buried in Sweet.

William Reed, Jr.

William, Jr., called Billy by his brothers and sisters, was the first child born at the South Fork cabin in August 1915. Like his brothers, he learned to hunt and trap, but his passion was fishing. His daughter Evie recalls that some of her family's best times involved fishing trips led by her father.

When the family moved to Sweet, Bill was often in charge of the cattle trips into High Valley. He would trail the cattle there in the spring and return with them in the fall. He inherited his mother's small stature and dark curly hair, but he had his father's blue eyes.

Bill left home early and went to work in the woods as a sawyer. While working in Oregon he met Hattie Louise Peters. They were married and moved back to Sweet where for a time they lived on the Nielson place and farmed for his parents. Following World War II, he and Hattie moved to Pinehurst, Idaho, and he went back to work as a sawyer. Then in 1964, he started work as a government trapper. He held this job until 1977, when he retired. He and Hattie stayed in Pinehurst until 1992, when they moved to Grangeville. Bill died a year later of lung cancer.

He and Hattie had three children—Jess, Lucille, and Evelynn. Bill loved to play cards, and taught all of his children his favorite games of poker, pinochle and solitaire, although he gave up poker after Hattie found religion. He also loved to tell stories. Although he was a man of few words, when it came to telling a good story, he could entertain his children for hours.

Sandy Reed

Sandy followed his brother Bill into the woods to become a logger. Born on the South Fork in 1917, he was twelve when the family settled in Sweet. Like his brothers, he enjoyed hunting and fishing.

Sandy was in Cascade working as a sawyer when he met Louise Chaffin, a pretty red-head. Together they had ten children: Myrna, Floyd, Earl, Sandy, Jr., Glen, Dale, Wayne, Ellen, Anna, and Robert.

When World War II broke out, Sandy enlisted, leaving Louise at home. After his discharge, he returned to Idaho and went back to work as a logger.

Although the link between alcoholism and heredity had not

been determined in the 1940s, Bessie always worried that this trait would be passed on from her side of the family. Her fears came true in Sandy, who squandered his pay checks at the local tavern every Friday night. Louise eventually tired of it, and left him in the late 1950s.

Sandy never remarried and never conquered his drinking problem. He died at the Idaho State Veteran's Home in Boise in November 1993.

Rose Mae Reed Swander

Rose, along with Mabel, took on many of the everyday tasks of the Reed household: cooking, cleaning, washing clothes, milking cows. She seldom complained. She was usually good natured and got along well with her father, unless he lost his temper. Then she could not accept how mean he could be. She was also extremely disappointed that he would not let her go on to high school.

Rose had a deep respect for all living things, a trait that started early on the South Fork. She loved animals and was never without a pet. As a child she was known to pack chipmunks around in her pockets, and in her later years she made pets out of magpies, orioles, and blue birds, along with a menagerie of calves, kittens, and dogs.

Like Mabel, Rose was also shy, preferring her family to outside social functions. She was also very prim and proper. However, her home became a haven for family members, as she hosted many of the holiday dinners, opened her door to brother Sam when he needed a place, and never turned anyone away hungry.

In her teens, Rose fell in love with Everett Swander, whose parents owned the ranch adjacent to the Reed's in Sweet. When the war broke out, Everett enlisted. Rose followed him to Florida

Rose worked in a rubber factory during World War II.

and California, traveling and staying with Mabel, before returning home to Sweet. When Everett was discharged in Seattle on Christmas Eve, 1945, Rose was there to meet him. The two were married that day. He would later tell his friends and family that she was the best Christmas gift he ever received.

The two returned to Sweet and Everett's boyhood home, staying there for a short time before purchasing a ranch of their own, adjacent to Everett's parents. The ranch provided a good home for their seven children: Anita, Alberta, Everett, Claudia, Edward, Gail Dean, and Lonnie.

In 1960, Rose suffered a serious head injury when she fell from her horse. She never fully recovered, and for the rest of her life, she suffered from severe headaches.

In the late 1970s, Rose and Everett left Sweet and moved to Emmett for a short time before before buying a place on the Little Salmon River between New Meadows and Riggins. It had been Rose's dream to return to the mountains she loved. They lived there until Everett's death in 1988. Rose then moved back to Emmett where she remained until her death in 1997.

Penn Reed

Penn was born on the South Fork in 1920 and left home shortly after the family moved into the Hamilton place in Sweet. Of all the Reed children, he had the most difficult time dealing with his father. For some reason, Reed tormented him until Penn had no choice but to leave. At just twelve, he traveled to Long Valley where he went to work for a rancher. From there he wandered the country for a time, riding the rails in the late 1930s before eventually returning to the Emmett area where he went to work in the timber industry.

During World War II, he moved to Seattle where he met his first wife Thelma Neshem. They returned to Emmett in the 1940s, and Penn went back to work as a logger.

Penn was a gentle, giving man, willing to help anyone in need. When Thelma's sister Doris needed a place to escape an abusive husband, Penn took her in. Doris later left, leaving her two children, Rick and Sharon, behind. Penn raised them, even after Thelma divorced him. He did the best he could providing for them and making sure they got an education. Although Penn never officially adopted the two children, they still refer to him as their father.

Penn, like his brothers, was an avid sportsman who enjoyed hunting, fishing, and trapping.

In the 1960s, Penn married Bessie Carey Cronk. They, along with Sam, bought a small farm in Emmett, and Penn built a new

Penn visiting his parents on the Sweet farm

house. He worked in the woods until his retirement, and then kept himself busy with his farm where they remained until their deaths. Bessie died in 1990 and Penn followed in August 1991. Both are buried in Sweet.

Margaret Marie Reed Tetro

Margaret (Marge) was born on the South Fork in 1922. She was the tallest of all the girls, and one of the most outspoken when it came to discussing her father and his behavior. While she was never really afraid of him, in her late teens she was very bitter toward her father because of the way he lived and his biased opinions.

Marge was attending the church revival when her brothers brought the tent down around her. Undaunted, Marge went on to become a strong member of the church. Although her father would not let her go on to high school, she steadfastly held to her dream to become a missionary. Throughout her teens she raised and saved money by selling eggs, and when she turned eighteen, she left home to fulfill her goal.

She first traveled to Montana and then to Seattle where she enrolled in the Northwest Bible Institute. Because of her lack of schooling, she struggled, but she managed to graduate. She later told her family that she was totally unprepared for life in the city. While she could milk a cow and make cottage cheese, she was totally unfamiliar with such items as a vacuum cleaner, a bicycle, and a bowling ball.

In 1943, she received her first appointment as a missionary and was sent to Ketchikan, Alaska. The following year she married Frank Tetro, Jr., who at the time was in the military. In 1945, Frank was transferred to Oregon where they remained until he was discharged. Then the couple moved to Los Angeles where Frank became a missionary. In 1950, they were sent to Japan where they would spend much of their next twenty-five years performing various church duties. Through all of this they had five children: Darlene, Frank III, Daisy, Dolores, and John.

In the fall of 1975, they returned to the United States. Marge spent time with her mother in Emmett during the last months of her life. After Bessie's death, they moved to California. They made one more trip to Japan before settling in Riggins, Idaho, in 1987 where Frank served as a minister. In 1993 they returned to Emmett.

With failing health, both Frank and Marge moved to an assisted care facility in Meridian. Frank died in 2001. Marge remains there as of this writing, where she helps other patients and runs a Bible study group, continuing the ministry she loved so much. She was against the publication of any book about her father, in accordance with her mother's wishes.

Anne Narcissus Reed Larson

The ninth child, Anne was born on the South Fork in February 1924. She has little memory of her time there. However, she does remember moving many times once the family reached Sweet. She also has vivid memories of the hard work on the farm, and at an early age, she vowed never to marry a farmer or a cowboy.

Anne was so small as a child that she did not start school until she was eight years old. She learned quickly, however, and was allowed to skip two grades. She eventually graduated from the eighth grade at fourteen and at the head of her class. She was extremely angry that her father did not allow her to go on to high school. To make up for it, she took jobs baby sitting in Emmett. The people she met there introduced her to libraries and night classes, so she was able to continue her education on her own.

Anne was one of the first Reed children to meet her grandmother, Mary Warren. She remembers her mother was a nervous wreck on that first meeting, afraid that Anne would break something in the Warren's home.

When she was sixteen she moved to Boise and took classes dealing with airplane mechanics and typing. From there, she moved to Spokane where she was employed by the Spokane Army Air Depot. In Spokane she had the time of her life. She lived in a grand house with other girls who were training to be nurses. Her host loved to entertain and sponsored dances at the old Davenport Hotel, one of the most prestigious places in the city at that time.

When her job at the Air Depot ended, Anne returned to

Emmett for a short period before moving to Seattle. She hired on with Boeing Aircraft as a stenographer and stayed there for six years. During that time she attended night classes at Broadway High School and earned her GED.

Anne met her husband in a bar in Seattle where she had gone with two of her friends. Norm Larson had just returned from military service in Europe, and according to Anne, she was the one who picked Norm out of the crowd. People who know Anne admit that she was never shy. They married in 1947 and had three sons: Garry, David, and Chris. While Anne told Norm of her early life on the South Fork and Sweet, she never took him home to meet her father.

Norm went to work for a record company. As part of his job, they traveled the country from Hawaii to Florida meeting celebrities of all kinds. They moved to California in 1968 where they both became avid golfers, a sport they picked up while living in Seattle.

Anne and Norm returned to Idaho in 1992 and settled in Meridian where Anne reconnected with her brothers and sisters. She was a special caregiver for them, visiting them regularly in the nursing homes and hospitals during their last days.

Today, Anne and Norm are still active. They spend their days playing bridge and gin rummy, with an occasional golf game on the side.

Nora Cecelia Reed Brooks

If Reed had a favorite daughter, it may have been Nora, who never backed down to a challenge. Born in March 1926, she received all of her education in Sweet. It was her job to keep track of Jim and Ruth on their two mile walk to school.

Anne described Nora as a "real pistol," who would speak her mind whenever she wanted. The two girls looked a lot alike, wore the same size as children, and according to Anne were the "best of buddies." They were inseparable during their years in Sweet and later in Seattle.

Nora graduated from the eighth grade in Sweet when she was fourteen. She moved to Emmett where her teacher got her a job doing housework. She then went to work at Spero's Drug Store in Emmett.

In the 1940s, she left to join Anne in Seattle. Before she departed, her father gave her his derringer, a gun he had carried with him since his Alaska days. According to Reed, Nora and Ruthie "were the only girls with nerve enough to use it." Since Ruthie was still at home and would not need it, the gun was passed to Nora.

Anne and Nora in front of the drug store where Nora worked

Once in Seattle, Nora went to work as a riveter and then found a job at Owl Drug. Working as a pharmacist there was Everett Brooks; he did not have a chance against Nora who, on the day they met, predicted they would marry. They remained in Seattle until 1953 and had three children: Robert, Janet, and James. Then they moved to Davenport, Washington where they bought their own drug store. They worked side by side for over twenty years.

Once in Davenport, Nora became an EMT. One of her more enjoyable tasks was taking her ambulance to the nearby Spokane Reservation where she would help deliver the babies of the Indian mothers who often refused to go to the hospital.

Nora and Everett enjoyed camping and boating; they especially loved spending time on the Oregon coast.

In 1982, Nora was diagnosed with ovarian cancer. While she put up a good fight, she could not overcome the disease and died in 1986.

James Marion Reed

The last Reed son, Jim, was born in a tent on the shores of Newell Lake near Montour in 1930. He was the most educated of the boys attending school on a regular basis in Sweet. He attended Montour High School for one year, where he played football. When the school closed and the students were transferred to Emmett, Jim quit school. He knew he would not be able to stay after school for football practice, so he saw no use to continue.

As the last son at home, much of the responsibility of the farm chores fell to him. But he ached to get out on his own and, at sixteen, joined his brothers in the timber industry. He worked there for a short time before returning to Emmett in 1948 where he managed a tavern and kept an eye out for his parents.

Jim was particularly close to Ruth. Since they were the last two children at home, they shared the responsibilities after Bessie went to work. Jim was also the protector of his little sister. While Bessie and Reed kept a tight rein on the other girls, Ruth was able to go anywhere as long as Jim was with her.

In the 1950s Jim joined the Marines and was sent to Korea where he fought on the front lines. The experience haunted him, and later in his life he would have nightmares about it.

Jim Reed with his father's pistol

After the war he returned to Emmett where he married Shirley Rose in 1954. They lived in Emmett, and he went to work in the lumber mill. He also helped out at his family's farm, especially after Bessie had her heart attack.

Jim held a succession of jobs in the 1950s and 60s. He worked as a hunting guide, was employed at the Hell's Canyon Dam, and then returned to Emmett to work in the lumber mill.

He and Shirley divorced in 1957. They had one son, Randy. Jim later married Sandra Corbett and they had three children: Susie, Russell, and Tracy.

In the the 1970s, Jim and his family moved to Oregon. He tried mining and then went to work on a ranch. They eventually moved to Sisters, Oregon, where he became the manager of a dude ranch.

In the spring of 1983, Jim was diagnosed with stomach cancer. He died July 1, 1983.

Ruth Ellen Reed Beckett

The baby of the family, Ruth, was born in April 1932. She has vivid memories of life with her older brothers and sisters before they moved away. According to Ruthie, as she was called by her family, she must have been a "brat." She remembers being spoiled by Mabel and crying to get her way with Marge. But life for Ruth was not easy. After all the children had left home, the burden of the chores and caring for her father fell on her.

Ruth was very small for her age, so small that she and her father fought over when she could start school. In the summer of 1938, even though she was six and ready for first grade, Reed told her she had to be able to walk two and one-half miles and weigh thirty pounds to go to school. When school started, Ruth could easily handle the walk, but she only weighed twenty-seven pounds. However, she pestered him, and he finally allowed her to go.

She excelled in school. While Reed did not want her to go on to high school, she did anyway. That was a pattern in Ruth's life: while her father forbade her to do many things, she did them anyway.

When Bessie went to work, Ruth had to take care of her father. By that time, Reed was in his seventies and, according to

Ruth, fairly easy to get along with. Still she had to get up early each morning, fix his breakfast, milk the cows, get to school, return home to fix his dinner, and then milk the cows again. In the summer, instead of school, she worked at the fruit packing plant in order to earn money for school clothes and books.

Ruth was seventeen when she met Bill Beckett at a basketball game in Boise. They eloped four months later. They moved to Seattle where they both worked for Boeing until Bill joined the Navy. Ruth stayed with Anne before joining Bill in San Diego where they had their first child, Kathy. When Bessie had her heart attack, Ruth and Kathy returned to Sweet to take care of her, and they remained while Bill was overseas. After Reed was sent to Blackfoot, they returned to San Diego, taking Bessie with them.

After Bill's discharge, they returned to Emmett to manage the Reed farm, but could not make a go of it. After the birth of their son Aaron in 1956, they returned to Seattle where Bill was rehired by Boeing. After only a few months there, they were forced to return to Emmett after Aaron developed asthma due to Seattle's damp climate.

Back in Emmett, Bill went to work overseeing an orchard, and then hired on as the manager of the Triple H Land & Cattle Company. The family participated in one of the last big cattle drives in the area, trailing cattle from Squaw Butte to High Valley.

In 1958 daughter Laura was born, and in 1960 Ruth and her family moved to Tennessee. Bill went to work for an implement company, and then supervised a commercial dry cleaning plant. He was so successful there that he was sent to Ireland to establish another operation, leaving Ruth and the children on their own. When he returned to the United States, he managed a chair factory. He quit the business in 1981, but in 1982 he was rehired and sent to Mexico City to establish a plant there. This

Ruth on the ranch in Sweet

time, Ruth accompanied him, and while neither one spoke any Spanish, they got along fine. Bill left the business after their return to the states, and together they began managing RV parks. They worked in North Carolina and West Virginia before staying in Florida for ten years. As for Ruth, she worked much of her life doing clerical work and helping her husband with his different businesses. They were a successful pair.

Bessie spent many of her last years with Ruth, helping out with the children as Ruth worked. Bessie felt needed, and Ruth really enjoyed having her. She was extremely happy when her mother was able to travel and spend quality time with her children in her later years.

As of this writing, Ruth and Bill still live in Tennessee. Bill has become a silversmith, and the two travel the country displaying his work. Ruth fills in at the day care at her church, and although she has been asked to work full time, she prefers her freedom. The grit and determination that characterized her as a child still hold true today.

Acknowledgments

Bessie Reed did not want the stories of Deadshot to be told. She wanted him to be remembered as a good husband and provider, and she was afraid that any book written would ignore this side of him. What Bessie did not realize is that any story about Reed is really a story about her. Their lives were intertwined, and one cannot write the history of Deadshot without including the courage and determination of his wife and children. The Reed family is a part of Idaho history and, because of that, their story needs to be told. I feel honored to have been given that opportunity.

First and foremost, I have to thank Alberta Smith, granddaughter of William and Bessie Reed, for entrusting me with the story. The encouragement and support of Alberta and her husband Duane made the project enjoyable.

Much credit must also go to Alberta's sister, Claudia Swander. Claudia envisioned a book about her grandfather over ten years ago and spent countless hours trying to make that book a reality. Claudia worked closely with Sheila Reddy, who did extensive research and wrote a preliminary manuscript about Reed. Their research, along with tape recordings that Claudia collected, were essential to the creation of this book.

It is a daunting task to recreate the life of someone as mysterious as William Reed. Trying to piece together his history from the tangled maze of tales he told was not only difficult but also exasperating at times. It was also difficult to bring Bessie into the picture. While she is a major figure in the story, so much of her life was behind the scenes that she resided forever in the shadows of her infamous husband.

Had it not been for Anne Reed Larson and Ruth Reed Beckett, the story of Deadshot and Bessie would have been impossible to write. Both were extremely honest and open when discussing their lives with me, and I admire them both. Ruth, in particular, was invaluable. Her input is on every page, and I appreciate all the time she devoted to this project so I could write the story. Working with her was truly a gift.

Many other people contributed to the creation of this book. Jim Bacon provided information about trapping, and Larry Kingsbury opened his files for me to research the South Fork homesteads. I also appreciate the company of Marquita Blanton, who traveled with me to the old Reed Ranch and entertained me with her own back country stories.

As for the actual production of the book, Tom Stewart worked his digital magic to restore many of the older photos. For the cover, Ellen McKinney offered much needed artistic advice. I also appreciated Frances Ford, my editor, who was always on the lookout for any split infinitives or dangling modifiers. A special thanks goes to Meagan McMahan who proofread the final draft. Finally, I thank my husband Bob who encourages me in all that I do. I would be lost without him.

Bibliography

Books and Manuscripts

Arrington, Leonard J. *History of Idaho.* Volume 1. Moscow: University of Idaho Press, 1994.

Beckett, Ruth Reed. *Family Memories of Ruth Reed Beckett.* Unpublished Manuscript.

Carrey, Johnny and Cort Conley. *The Middle Fork: A Guide.* Cambridge, Idaho: Backeddy Books, 1992.

Colson, Art. *Rewards of Rage.* Middleton, Idaho: CHJ Publishing, 1997.

Conley, Cort. *Idaho for the Curious.* Cambridge, Idaho: Backeddy Books, 1982.

Ellis, Marietta. "Colonial Soap Making. Its History and Techniques." The Soap Factory. 2 Jan. 2003 <http://www. alcasoft.com/soapfact/history.html>.

Illustrated History of North Idaho. San Francisco/Spokane: Western Historical Publishing Company, 1903.

Johns, Joshua. "Buffalo Bill's Wild West Show." Nov. 1995. American Studies University of Virginia. 20 April 2002 <http://xroads.virginia.edu/~HYPER/HNS/BUFFALO BILL/home.html>.

Preston, Peter. *An Outline of the Cultural History of the Frank Church River of No Return Wilderness.* McCall: Payette National Forest Heritage Program, 2001.

Reddy, Sheila D. *Deadshot The Reed Legacy*. Unpublished Manuscript.

Sayers, Isabelle S. *Annie Oakley and Buffalo Bill's Wild West*. New York: Dover Publications, 1981.

Wilkins, Frederick. *The Law Comes to Texas: The Texas Rangers from 1870-1901*. Austin: State House Press, 1999.

Woods, Sheldon, ed. *Valley County, Idaho: Prehistory to 1920*. Donnelly, Idaho: Valley County History Project, 2001.

Newspapers

The Cascade News. Cascade, Idaho.
Jan. 18, 1918 June 27, 1919 July 4, 1919

Clearwater Republican. Orofino, Idaho. Jan. 2, 1913.

Clearwater Tribune. Orofino, Idaho.
Mar. 4, 1943 June 3, 1943 June 24, 1943
Sept. 30, 1943 Oct. 13, 1943 Oct. 21, 1943
Jan. 13, 1943

Emmett Index. Emmett, Idaho.
Oct. 17, 1929 Nov. 21, 1909 Nov. 20, 1930
June 23, 1932

Idaho Statesman. Boise, Idaho. Oct. 12, 1927.

Lewiston Morning Tribune. Lewiston, Idaho.
Aug. 4, 1908 Aug. 5, 1908 Aug. 6, 1908
Aug. 7, 1908 Aug. 19, 1908 Sept. 4, 1908
Sept. 5, 1908 Sept. 6, 1908 Sept. 10, 1908
Sept. 11, 1908 Sept. 12, 1908 Jan. 22, 1909
Jan. 27, 1909 Jan. 28, 1909 Jan. 31, 1909
Feb. 7, 1909 Feb. 12, 1909

Nampa Leader Herald. Nampa, Idaho. Nov. 8, 1930.

Pierce City Miner. Pierce, Idaho.

June 5, 1908	July 24, 1908	Aug. 7, 1908
Aug. 14, 1908	Nov. 20, 1908	Feb. 5, 1909
Feb. 26, 1909	Mar. 5, 1909	May 7, 1909
May 14, 1909	May 21, 1909	May 28, 1909
July 30, 1909	Aug. 18, 1909	Aug. 27, 1909
Sept. 24, 1909	May 19, 1911	July 14, 1911

Federal Census Records

The following records were found at the Idaho State Historical Library and Archives in Boise, Idaho.

Idaho: 1880, 1900, 1910, 1920, 1930.

Texas: 1880, 1900.

About the Author

Kathy Deinhardt Hill is the author of two previous books which feature Idaho history. Her first, *Spirits of the Salmon River,* published by Backeddy Books, documents the lives of sixty people buried on the Salmon River. Her second book, *On the Road, Twenty Great Day Trips from McCall,* published by Big Mallard Books, is a travel guide which details the history of areas near McCall, Idaho.

Index

M

N

O

P

R

S

Order Form

Name____

Mailing Address ________________________________

City, State,Zip__________________________________

Quantity			Total
	For Better or Worse	$12.95	
	On the Road	$12.95	
	Spirits of the Salmon River	$13.95	
		subtotal	
		Idaho Sales Tax (5%)	
		Shipping and handling ($1.00 per book)	
		Total	

Send Check or Money Order Payable to:
Big Mallard Books
14068 Pioneer Road
McCall, Idaho 83638